web3 requires boldness. Litman's bc ___ tools to thrive in this new era. Let's dig in and build together!

Erika Wykes-Sneyd, Global Vice President and GM of adidas /// studio

Future innovators must embrace web3. This book simplifies these concepts, making them easy to grasp and exciting. A must-have for the new generation of brand leaders!

Sebastian Oddo, Global Digital Marketing Innovation

Litman's book is essential reading for anyone looking to understand and thrive in the web3 and NFT frontier. Its accessible approach to complex concepts makes it a must-read for future innovators.

Ramzi Chaabane, Global Category Manager, L'Oréal

It doesn't matter what you thought you knew about NFTs, code is law and they are a core part of the future of the internet. This book is a useful must-read for anyone starting their journey in web3.

Jennifer Roebuck, CMO, Metaversal, Co-Founder, Tortilla

Digital ownership is the new paradigm. Litman outlines the value, need, and steps to succeed in this new world.

Mathew Sweezey, Chief Strategy Officer Smart Token Labs, Former Co-Founder Salesforce Web3 Studio

Following the hype cycles of the last decades web3 is no different. Value-adding use cases emerge post-hype. Litman's book helps navigate through the debris of the hype paving the way for sustainable business value in the future.

Nino Bergfeld, Retail Industry Advisor, Salesforce

Litman's knowledge bomb of insight, experience & innovation about the power of web3 and AI is one to enjoy. So many practitioners forget about the importance that brands play in technological progress but Litman weaves a wonderful story about where we have been but more crucially where we're going to.

JC Oliver, Founder, Move78

The blockchain is ushering in the new generation of gaming, entertainment, and the internet. Litman tackles the complexity and promise of the space with accessibility for all.

Sam Barberie, Head of Strategy and Partnerships, Sequence

Litman is as sharp a strategist as they come -- he not only knows where the puck is going, he knows how to show others the path there.

Brian Trunzo, VP & Global Head of BD, Polygon Labs

Having known Litman as one of the most insightful thinkers in emerging tech, this book is a game-changer for innovators looking to understand web3.

Matt Law, Chief Commercial Officer, Outlier Ventures

Litman consistently stays ahead of the curve as a trendsetter and forward thinker. This book encapsulates the multifaceted world of web3, from gaming and arts to business and community. It's a must-read for anyone looking to grasp the innovative concepts that are shaping the future.

Lucas Verra, Co-Founder, POAP Studio

GETTING STARTED WITH WEB3 AND NFTS

An introduction to virtual goods and tokenisation

Michael Litman

bcs

The
Chartered
Institute
for IT

Contents

About the author

TL;DR INTRO

Michael Litman is an award-winning emerging tech enthusiast, educator and evangelist with over 15 years of experience in digital brand communications. He founded a venture-backed tech startup, was named a 'Tech Pioneer' by BIMA 100 in 2023, and is globally recognised for his strategies and partnerships in innovation, web3 and emerging technologies.

DETAILED INTRODUCTION

Michael Litman is currently a London based senior director, emerging tech innovation strategy at Monks, a marketing and technology services provider with over 7,000 staff around the world.

He brings over 15 years of experience in digital communications, spanning PR, social media, advertising, consulting and the founding of a venture-backed video production and technology research startup.

He has since worked on or for some of the biggest brands, agencies and consultancies in the world, including the likes of R/GA, Poke, Dare, AnalogFolk and Contagious.

Litman is a collector at heart, digitally and physically, whether that is boards on Pinterest, print magazines, books, art, virtual goods, NFTs, AI tools, crypto, trainers and of course all things Nottingham Forest.

In June 2022, Litman had the great honour of curating his own art gallery exhibition of NFTs at Pier 17 in Manhattan, New York City as part of ApeFest during NFT NYC 2022.

A recognised thought leader at the intersection of creativity, community, culture and commerce, Litman received a 'Tech Pioneer' award by BIMA 100 in 2023. He is passionate about staying at the forefront of technology, navigating the complexities of AI, blockchain, web3 and digital trends, and advising global brands on how to be authentically culturally relevant within these spaces.

Litman has been featured in the '30 Most Creative Advertising People Under 30' by Business Insider in 2015, the 'Top 100 UK Entrepreneurs' by CityAM in 2016, the AdTech Shift 100 by KPMG in 2017 and the 'Top 50 in London Creative Tech' by TLA and the Creative Industries Federation in 2017. He was the first Head of Digital for Contagious, Consulting Strategy Director at R/GA (digital innovation agency of the year 2019) and was formerly Lead Creative Strategist at Monks (the most awarded digital production company) from 2019 to 2022.

Litman has been featured in *AdAge*, *The Drum*, *Wall Street Journal*, *Campaign Magazine*, *Business Insider*, *PSFK* and many more publications. He has been a keynote conference speaker and panellist at numerous conferences around the world including Adworld, Blockchain Barcelona, NFT NYC and a guest on a number of leading industry podcasts. Since early 2022, he has spent his time professionally in a broader, global innovation role.

Acknowledgements

It has been a lifelong passion of mine to be a collector of niche artefacts, starting out when I was much younger with Premier League football stickers. More recently, this collector habit became somewhat of a sneaker-collecting obsession and latterly collecting digital art and NFT projects. When I combine this with my professional skills as a researcher and strategist, I have found a sweet spot within emerging tech strategy. The web3 and NFT community is a passionate, energetic, always-on ecosystem that is largely of the belief that rising tides lift all ships.

First thank you goes to Kai Turner. A long-time friend, co-conspirator, side hustler and my entry point into all things web3 and NFT in 2021. Thank you for taking me under your wing and opening my eyes to what was at the time an entirely new space to me.

I have gathered additional insights for this book from experiences of peers, influencers, figureheads and brands.

I am incredibly grateful to my wife, Charlotte, who at the time of me writing this was both heavily pregnant and latterly bringing our first child into the world. Thank you for allowing me to go deep into this rabbit hole and successfully come out the other side as a father and author.

Finally, this book would not have been possible also without the continuous stewardship and drive of the BCS publishing team. Thank you for providing me with the opportunity to bring this out into the world as an encapsulation of the heady days within the space from 2021 to 2024 and my predictions for future outlooks in 2025 and beyond.

Introduction

Hello! My name is Michael Litman and firstly I would like to thank you for picking up this book, *'Getting started with web3 and NFTs: An introduction to virtual goods and tokenisation'*.

You might be curious and wondering whether you want to read on and find out what NFTs, virtual goods and tokenisation means! If so, my objective is to educate, to inform, to demystify, to shine a light and offer a helping hand to people entirely new to this fascinating and nascent space who are curious, want to find out more and be part of the web3 and NFT ecosystem. My aspiration is that this gives some reassurance, confidence, trust and insight into what may seem like a daunting and sometimes scary, off-putting and bamboozling topic.

I will come at the subject from two different perspectives: both professionally (as an educator, strategist and researcher) having worked at some of the largest creative communications agencies in the world over the past 15 years, and personally (as a collector, community member and culturally curious lover of new technology since as long as I can remember). This is definitely a trait that has been passed down from my father David Litman, who is a collector of rare stamps, whiskies, seashells and has Pinterest boards in the hundreds!

This book will be a chronology of how it all began, what it was like in the heady days of 2021, bringing us up to the present day in 2024 and beyond for what things might look like further out still. The year 2021 was a particularly rare set of market forces, when, due to a pandemic where everyone was limited to being at home, coupled with a stimulus check in America, crypto and NFTs burst onto the scene.

I am fascinated professionally about the intersection between creativity, community, culture and commerce, so you could say NFTs directly hits the bullseye between all of the above and why I have been so captivated by them for many years. It is at this intersection that NFTs really lit a fire in me when back in 2021, and coupled with a few years of knowledge in crypto, I found myself thrust into the NFT ecosystem in early 2021 via Kai Turner and Meebits DAO.

So, what is a non-fungible token (NFT) and why should you care? We will go into some of the technical aspects at an introductory level to set the foundations for what is to come. We will define NFT, blockchain, what a smart contract is and touch on interoperability and decentralisation.

1 What are NFTs and what is their significance in the digital world?

An NFT (non-fungible token) is a unique digital asset, sometimes referred to as a digital collectible, that first and foremost represents ownership or proof of authenticity of a specific item or piece of content. Imagine this being like your receipt or invoice when buying a high-value item. Instead, this 'receipt' will now live on the blockchain as proof that it can be traced back to you owning it.

The basic premise of the blockchain is that it is one big digital diary that keeps track of every transaction that is processed on it. It stores this data in a way that makes it difficult to alter, hack or game. Once a transaction is recorded on a blockchain, it becomes very difficult to change or delete. We will go into deeper technical detail towards the end of Chapter 1.

The 'non-fungible' aspect relates to it being unique, one of a kind and irreplaceable like-for-like with anything else. We may compare it to baseball trading cards. These are each individual and unique, and if you trade them for another card, you would be getting something completely different. This means it is non-fungible.

Conversely, cryptocurrency (a method of paying for digital goods) is fungible as if you were to trade some Bitcoin or Ethereum, you would be getting the same thing back.

Here follows a quick explainer on what Bitcoin and Ethereum are as these will be referenced in future chapters.

Bitcoin is a decentralised digital currency, created in 2009 by an anonymous entity known as Satoshi Nakamoto. It operates on a peer-to-peer network, allowing users to send and receive payments without the need for intermediaries like banks.

Ethereum is also a decentralised, open-source blockchain platform established by Vitalik Buterin in 2015. Unlike Bitcoin, which primarily functions as a digital currency, Ethereum is designed to facilitate smart contracts and decentralised applications (DApps).

In its simplest terms, if you imagine, for example, buying a new iPhone which out of the box is set to factory settings, that is seen as fungible because everyone is buying the same phone. As soon as you start using it and have your own photos, notes and personal information on it, that is seen to be unique and non-fungible.

Interoperability is another key concept. This involves the ability for different blockchain networks to communicate with each other, exchange data and conduct transactions seamlessly. If you buy a Sony PlayStation 5 console, you can only play games that are made for that console; you would not be able to buy a game for the Microsoft Xbox and play it on a Sony console because each console is a closed ecosystem and not interoperable. With the premise of interoperability, you would in theory be able to interchangeably play one game across two different consoles. In practice, things are a little more complicated.

When it comes to NFTs, many are created on standard blockchain protocols like Ethereum's ERC-721 or ERC-1155. This standardisation means that NFTs can be bought, sold or traded across various platforms and virtual environments.

The idea of smart contracts and programmability is also key. NFTs can have smart contracts that enable programmable features. For instance, an artist can program royalties into an NFT so that they receive a percentage of sales whenever their art is resold. Imagine a smart contract as a kind of automatic digital rulebook. It is a set of rules written in code that lives on the internet, specifically on a blockchain. This rulebook automatically makes sure that everyone follows the agreed rules without the need for a middleman, like a lawyer or a bank. Smart contracts are effectively digital contracts stored on a blockchain that are automatically acted upon when predetermined terms and conditions are met. They play a crucial role as when someone creates an NFT, a smart contract is used to record the 'ingredients' of the NFT. For example, the rarity and volume have a driving impact on the notion of value, whether it is a 1/1, meaning that it is the only one that exists, or one in a series of 100 or 1,000, which makes it still scarce but not as unique. If it is in a series, each will have different traits to ascertain its 'uniqueness' on the blockchain. Some collectors will search for pieces of art/collectibles as part of a collection that have particular traits which may be more desirable than others. The action of creating the smart contract for a project is known as 'minting'. The smart contract makes sure that the digital item is unique and it records who owns it. One of the more interesting things about these contracts is that they can also handle the transfer of an NFT from one person to another, which is how NFTs can be so easily bought and sold. The smart contract ensures that when an NFT is sold, the new owner is recorded, and the previous owner cannot claim it anymore. It is like having an automated system that keeps track of who owns what without any confusion.

Finally, an NFT can provide a history of ownership, proving the provenance of the digital asset. This is particularly valuable in the art world, where the authenticity and history of an artwork contribute significantly to its value. You can compare this to offline assets with the example of buying gold, jewellery or a watch, with which you will typically also receive a separate paper proof of ownership. From a collectibles aspect, there are now marketplaces such as StockX or even eBay that act as an authentication middleman to verify that what you are buying is not a replica or fake, whether that is clothing, trainers or other collectible items.

SIGNIFICANCE ON THE DIGITAL WORLD

The significance of NFTs on the digital world has been cemented over recent years through many tentpole moments in popular culture.

These include:

- CryptoKitties clogging up the Ethereum network at its height in 2017.
- CryptoPunks being launched in 2017 by Larva Labs as one of the earliest NFT generative art collections.
- Axie Infinity game being launched in March 2018.
- Art Blocks generative art platform being launched in November 2020.
- NBA Top Shots being one of the first major brands to create digital collectibles from sporting moments in 2021.
- Dmitri Cherniak creating generative art project Ringers using 1,000 different outputs in January 2021.
- Tyler Hobbs creating a generative art project Fidenza in June 2021.
- Beeple selling an NFT artwork for $69 million in 2021.
- Nike acquiring the NFT collectibles studio RTFKT for a rumoured $1 billion in December 2021.
- Bored Ape Yacht Club born April 2021.
- Adidas creating Into the Metaverse NFT project and generating $23 million of sales on launch day in 2021.
- Sotheby's and Christie's selling some of the most prominent, rare and culturally historic NFTs 2021–2024.
- CryptoPunks partnering with Tiffany on 250 custom pendants and selling out in 22 minutes in 2022.
- Gucci creating a limited supply of sterling silver necklaces based on a Yuga Labs Otherside 'koda' in 2023.

- Chrome Squiggle #8107 by Snowfro transcending generative art and selling 262 physical editions by Avant Arte in December 2023.

- Robert Alice creating an art piece in itself with Taschen through the gigantic book *On NFTs* released in 2024.

- Doodles creating their own feature film *Dullsville and the Doodleverse* launching end of 2024.

- Pudgy Penguins announcing in 2024 it has sold 1 million toy physical plushies in 12 months with Walmart in the USA and Meebits to have their own game world within Otherside launching in 2024.

We will explore this in more detail in Chapter 2 also relating to their impact on various industries.

BLOCKCHAIN

Let's dive back into blockchains. To recap, the basic premise is that a blockchain is one big digital diary that keeps track of every transaction that is processed on it. It stores this data in such a way that makes it difficult to alter, hack or game. Once a transaction is recorded on a blockchain, it becomes very difficult to change or delete. Each block contains a cryptographic hash of the previous block, creating a linked chain. Altering any information in a block would require altering all subsequent blocks, which is computationally impractical.

Unlike traditional databases managed by a central authority, a blockchain is known as being decentralised. It also operates without needing to trust any one centralised company or entity to keep it secure and accurate. Here, we need to grasp the difference between decentralised versus centralised entities in this context. Banks in the current system are the epitome of a centralised entity, meaning that they control all aspects of anything under their brand. For example, if you have a credit card, all operations are run within the company, such as a customer service number you can call and support you can get either online or from humans. However, decentralised entities refer to the transfer of control and decision-making from a centralised entity to a distributed network.

This ultimately provides enhanced security, transparency and efficiency compared to traditional centralised systems. A blockchain node is a device, usually a computer, that participates in a blockchain network. It runs the blockchain protocol's software, allowing it to help validate transactions and keep the network secure. The diary or ledger that the transactions are stored on is therefore maintained across a network of computers (nodes), making it less susceptible to control or manipulation by a single entity. Because every transaction is recorded and verified by multiple nodes (computers) in the network, blockchain technology also creates a greater sense of transparency and trust. Therefore it is a trustless and decentralised 'ledger' or diary. Participants can verify transactions independently and in real time. Everything is visible for everyone on the blockchain. Its potential extends beyond cryptocurrencies, offering solutions to various industries including manufacturing, healthcare, fashion, media and communications industries, though it also faces significant challenges.

NFTs have been moving rapidly past the first single-use case (digital art provenance) to a whole world of opportunity; the tokenisation of real-world assets in 2024 and beyond is going to continue to pick up traction and use cases. Storing digital copies (tokens) of real-world assets on the blockchain has the potential to fundamentally change and shape every industry as blockchain technology goes mainstream.

In summary, an NFT is a unique digital asset that represents ownership or proof of authenticity of a specific item. It all happens on the blockchain, which you can think of as one big decentralised diary that records all user transactions. NFT's impact and significance in the digital world has been strongly felt in recent years with the likes of CryptoKitties, NBA Top Shot, Art Blocks, Larva Labs, CryptoPunks, Bored Ape Yacht Club, RTFKT, Ringers and Fidenza to name a few, all cementing themselves in web3 pop culture and reaching somewhat iconic status already. Let's now take a look at the historical evolution of NFTs and their impact across industries.

2   The historical evolution of NFTs and their impact on various industries

Despite what many may believe, NFTs did not start with CryptoKitties, CryptoPunks, Avastars or Bored Ape Yacht Club. The first recorded NFT was a 2014 video created by Jennifer and Kevin McCoy, entitled Quantum.

> *How to picture the moment of creation. A spark, a seed, a particle. We have narratives that describe it as an interval of days or as a cryptic alphabet that divides the earth from the firmament. [Kevin McCoy's] Quantum takes its place alongside other original icons replacing their aura and gilding with a pulsating luminous heartbeat. To call this a mandala would not be an understatement, since what is a mandala if not an allegory for a universe, its revolutions, breath and winking into being out of nothingness?*[1]

Kevin McCoy, from Seattle, USA, studied Philosophy at university, and Jennifer McCoy, born in Sacramento, USA, did Theatre Arts and Film Studies. They met and started dating in Paris in 1990, where they went to relearn French theories on film and popular culture. They both went on to pursue a master's degree in Electronic Arts at the Rensselaer Polytechnic Institute in Upstate New York. In 1996, the couple moved to New York. Since 2022, Kevin McCoy has been an Associate Professor in the Department of Art and Art Professions at NYU, while Jennifer is a Professor in the Art Department at Brooklyn College. Their website includes over 150 exhibitions that the artists have collaborated on. Over 50 press features are listed

---

1   Alice, R. (2021) *A Quantum Leap: Kevin McCoy's Genesis NFT, Medium*. Available at: https://studiorobertalice.medium.com/a-quantum-leap-kevin-mccoys-genesis-nft-db7c93f5094d.

there, dating back to 2000. They received 13 awards, such as the 2005 Visual Artist of the Year from *Wired Magazine* in San Francisco. Most recently, Kevin McCoy received the 2022 Webby Lifetime Achievement Award for developing what we now know as NFTs, alongside the American tech executive and writer Anil Dash, who bought the first ever NFT for only $4!

Quantum represents a combination of 179 different frames. The main object represented in the video is an octagon filled with various coloured objects, such as circles and arcs, among others. Some shapes are larger than others, surround smaller ones and pulsate hypnotically in a luminous manner.

> *This code-driven work presents an ongoing, abstract cycle of birth, death, and rebirth. It tells this story through color, line and movement. In 2014, I had an idea to use blockchain technology to create indelible provenance and ownership of digital images of this kind. Quantum was the first ever to be recorded in this way.*[2]

What was the use case for doing so? Because they wanted to develop a way to sell the piece in its digital form. The problem Kevin encountered was establishing the provenance of a digital piece of art.

Provenance in art typically denotes the authentication of the creator, the content and the ownership history; at the time, there was no way to do this. McCoy thought this would be a problem for more people than just himself and Jennifer, so they teamed up with Anil Dash to solve the problem of digital provenance. It was at this point that they began to explore blockchain technology to see if this would be the path forward. What they wanted to create was purely a platform where artists could have control over their work, which means to claim ownership and earn money.

The first ever NFT was introduced during a live presentation for the Seven on Seven conference in New York in 2014 and represented an important event in the history of NFTs. At this

---

2   Tech (2023) *The first NFT ever and where it is now. DigitalArtists' Blog.* Available at: www.digitalartists.com/blog/first-nft-ever/.

event, McCoy and Dash came up with the idea of monetised graphics, what is now known as an NFT. It would work by linking a non-fungible/replaceable blockchain marker to a specific work of art through on-chain metadata using the blockchain Namecoin. At this event, Dash bought the first NFT, Quantum, for only $4.

Interestingly, Quantum was forgotten for a long time following its 2014 mint. This was largely due to its original home on Namecoin, a pre-Ethereum Bitcoin offshoot. Specifically, Quantum lived on Namecoin Block 174923, minted on 2 May 2014 at 21:27:34 and that is where it stayed for years – until the 2021 NFT bull market and a new era dawned. When NFTs started to gain mainstream attention and sell for millions of dollars in 2021, McCoy realised he might be sitting on a golden egg. So, he started to promote Quantum, turning to media outlets like Axios to discuss his work and its role in NFT history. Thanks largely to this publicity push, their fortunes and lives changed immeasurably.

Fast forward to 2021, and Sotheby's, one of the world's largest brokers of fine and decorative art, jewellery and collectibles, was the seller of Quantum, which by then was already seven years old. The auction 'Natively Digital' only lasted for a week. There was no pre-sale value but it had reached a bid of $140,000 on its first day. The final bid was by anonymous collector Sillytuna for $1.47 million. In the same auction, Sillytuna sold CryptoPunk #7523 'Covid Alien' from his own collection for $11.8 million.[3]

In the long timeline of art, there are few works that serve as genesis blocks to their own chain of history. They are seismic forks in direction; forks that usher in new movements that block by block, mint by mint, usher in new art histories. These works close chapters on the art histories that came before,

---

3 *Quantum: Natively Digital: A curated NFT Sale: 2021* (no date) *Sotheby's.* Available at: www.sothebys.com/en/buy/auction/2021/natively-digital-a-curated-nft-sale-2/ quantum.

while anchoring a new flowering of human creativity. These prime movers occupy a singular position in art history. They came first. Kevin McCoy's Quantum is such a work. [...] And if blockchains stand as the Gutenberg Bible of the 21st century, then how do we prize the first of these records? In my view, Quantum will always be the most historically important work in the history of NFTs.[4]

The idea behind NFTs was, and is, profound. Technology should be enabling artists to exercise control over their work, to more easily sell it, to more strongly protect against others appropriating it without permission. By devising the technology specifically for artistic use, McCoy and I hoped we might prevent it from becoming yet another method of exploiting creative professionals. But nothing went the way it was supposed to. Our dream of empowering artists hasn't yet come true, but it has yielded a lot of commercially exploitable hype.[5]

In 10 years looking back, if in fact these are to grow, this piece can represent and symbolize the start of something that is quite revolutionary and very impactful.[6]

In summary, while many think of their favourites such as CryptoKitties, NBA TopShot or Bored Ape Yacht Club, to name but a few, as being the earliest memories and originators, the fact that a relatively unknown couple were the true pioneers of this whole movement, selling it initially for just $4, shows us two things:

1. The old trope of 'we're still early' persists, even in 2024.
2. Everything has moved on, progressed and developed onwards by orders of magnitude since 2014 and some 10 years later to the present day.

---

4 Alice, R. (2021) A Quantum Leap: Kevin McCoy's Genesis NFT, Medium. Available at: https://studiorobertalice.medium.com/a-quantum-leap-kevin-mccoys-genesis-nft-db7c93f5094d.

5 Dash, A. (2021) *NFTs weren't supposed to end like this*, The Atlantic. Available at: www.theatlantic.com/ideas/archive/2021/04/nfts-werent-supposed-end-like/618488/.

6 *Sotheby's sells first NFT that sparked a craze* (2021) *France 24*. Available at: www.france24.com/en/live-news/20210604-sotheby-s-sells-first-nft-that-sparked-a-craze.

3 What are NFT marketplaces, and what is their role and the process of buying, selling and trading NFTs?

It is fair to say that the NFT marketplaces in use have experienced their own 'metas' just like the ebbs and flows of projects, memecoins, crypto and even the economy itself. If we take a trip back to 2021–2022, OpenSea was, by a significant distance, the number one marketplace for NFTs. It had been building up to this point for a number of years, being founded in 2017, rapidly gaining recognition and market share. It has raised over $400 million in venture capital from some of the biggest outfits like Andreessen Horowitz and Paradigm as well as high profile celebrities.

It was the world's first web3 marketplace for NFTs and crypto collectibles. Users could browse, create, buy, sell and auction NFTs using OpenSea. It is also a non-custodial platform, allowing users full control and access to their cryptocurrency wallets. Users interact directly with each other to buy or sell NFTs individually or in bundles.

Yet in truth, the moat they built as the five-year overnight success story in the heady days of 2021 was not as unique as many had thought and hoped, with myriad NFT marketplaces broadly all doing a similar job. Critically, it is eyeballs, volume of transactions and sentiment that matter and as soon as those start to wander elsewhere, it is a much steeper challenge to bring them back to your playground. OpenSea CEO, Devin Finzer confirms this in an interview with TechCrunch:

Customers come for the product experience initially, then stick around if the product continues to meet their needs and continues to improve alongside the evolution of the space. We still have so much further to go in terms of representing all of the wide array of things that NFTs can represent.[7]

Marketplaces generally are online platforms where NFTs are bought, sold and traded. In exchange for a fee, the NFT marketplace will typically handle the transfer of an NFT from one party to the other. Think of them as an eBay for NFTs. As such, these digital marketplaces play a crucial role in the NFT ecosystem by providing a space for creators to list their NFTs and for collectors to browse and purchase them.

Finzer is most excited about web3 gaming and 'physical items represented as NFTs', predicting that these will be prominent use cases in 2024 and beyond.

If you look at existing marketplaces for rare physical sneakers, that's actually quite vibrant; there's a whole community of people that like to buy and sell those sorts of physical things . . . So one of the really cool use cases for entities is you take a physical pair of sneakers, you create an NFT, [and] you can buy and sell that NFT as many times as it can move around from person to person before it is actually redeemed for the physical item.

It is not just about art and profile pictures. It is really about representing all sorts of different things on-chain . . . and then some things that we haven't even imagined yet.[8]

The NFT marketplace ecosystem included NBA Top Shots, Binance, Nifty Gateway, Rarible, CryptoPunks, Superrare, KnownOrigin (acquired by eBay), Looksrare, Crypto.com, Mintable, Zora, Foundation, Makersplace, fxhash and Coinbase NFT (briefly).

---

7 *TechCrunch is part of the Yahoo family of brands* (2024) *Yahoo!* Available at: https://techcrunch.com/2024/02/08/opensea-david-finzer-interview/

8 Ibid.

According to data aggregator site CryptoSlam, on 1 January 2022, NFT global sales volume had reached $23.77 billion. In 2023, that dropped to $8.7 billion and at the time of writing, it stands at $5.22 billion in Q1 2024.

At the time of writing and over the past 30 days, according to Dappradar data, OpenSea is in fifth place behind OKX (fourth), Unisat (third), Magic Eden (second) and Blur (first). From being valued at $13.3 billion in 2022 and fast forwarding to November 2023, where 50 per cent of all staff were confirmed to be laid off, in reporting by Decrypt, it has been a rollercoaster few years of high highs and low lows for OpenSea. OpenSea had previously laid off roughly 20 per cent of its staff in July 2022, leaving it with a workforce of 230 employees, The Information reported.

Finzer said in the announcement:

Today [November 3rd 2023], we are making significant organizational and operating changes as we focus on building a more nimble and ultimately better – version of OpenSea. With these changes, we are better positioned to deliver for the community, shipping high-impact efforts and matching the speed at which this space evolves.[9]

Why did OpenSea lose market share? It became complacent, did not continue to innovate, improve on user experience and interface, move to where interest was shifting, simplify the complex, adapt and evolve while other smaller, more nimble new entrants did. Royalties and the removal of these on sales on OpenSea also became a big issue which Magic Eden pounced on by introducing a royalty-supportive marketplace in collaboration with Yuga Labs.

---

9 Hayward, A. (2023) *OpenSea slashes NFT Marketplace staff by 50%, Decrypt.* Available at: https://decrypt.co/204371/opensea-slashes-nft-marketplace-staff-50-layoffs.

There are parallels between OpenSea and the crypto wallet MetaMask, too, which has seen many more competitors enter the wallet space. MetaMask is the world's leading self-custody web3 platform with 30 million monthly active users. Developed by Consensys, MetaMask is one of the most known crypto wallets, which is used to mint and collect NFTs, join DAOs, play games and participate in DeFi protocols. It commanded strong dominance and a monopolistic share of the wallet space, which is now more diluted in 2024. At the time of their greatest dominance, there was a lot of noise and endless scrutiny that they would both create and distribute their own tokens, which would reward users and create liquidity moments, for example, $SEA and $MASK. This has not happened and it does not seem likely.

However, Magic Eden saw the opportunity with this want and need from users, making great strides of its own in building its market share by promising to do just that. On 29 February 2024, Magic Eden announced an 'ETH OG Diamond Claim' would be coming in March 2024. It would go all the way back to purchases on Ethereum since 2017.[10] This was a big moment as it did not require any time-consuming and onerous tasks like farming/mining/grinding leaderboards for rewards; it was a retroactive giving back to anyone who had bought NFTs from 2017 to 2024. However, this did end up disappointing when some ended up getting a very low amount of diamonds compared to the $ value spent over the duration of time their wallet has been active.

On the wallet side, Rainbow, Phantom, Rabby, Coinbase, Solfare and many more have seen the wallet market become a lot more congested and competitive. In February 2024, Consensys revealed that in terms of monthly active users (MAUs) for MetaMask, it saw +55 per cent growth between September 2023 and January 2024, climbing from 19 million to over 30 million. According to the release, this growth nearly matches

---

10 Magic Eden (2024) X. 29th February. Available at: https://twitter.com/MagicEden/ status/1763218489018343831.

the peak figures seen during January 2022, when it counted 31.7 million monthly active users, up from 10 million users in August 2021. As Dan Finlay, Chief Ethos Officer at Consensys and MetaMask Co-founder, said:

More broadly, web3 has seen significant signals of mainstream adoption with an increasingly strong regulatory, workforce and technical foundation, and growing regulatory certainty in jurisdictions such as the UK, EU and Hong Kong [...] As we witness the growth of MetaMask and the broader web3 ecosystem, we understand that the foundation of this expansion is user trust and security. The integration of advanced, privacy-preserving security alerts is a game-changer in protecting our users from the threats of phishing and hacking. By proactively preventing malicious transactions, we're not just enhancing security, we're empowering our users to navigate the web3 space with greater confidence. This is a crucial step towards ensuring that MetaMask remains at the forefront of secure, self-custodial crypto wallets for both new and experienced users.[11]

It is worth also noting that the continued proliferation of chains and the growing attention being paid to them has also grown exponentially over the years. This has impacted where both time and money are being spent. Where previously, NFTs were primarily being traded in Ethereum, the interest is now across Blast and its gamified farming/mining jackpot approach, Solana, Base by Coinbase, Bitcoin and Ordinals. Fantasy Top trading cards was a brief phenomenon in 2024 (on ETH), which did more volume specifically in May 2024 than all Ethereum NFTs combined.

---

[11] *MetaMask reveals 55% surge in users, introduces default security alerts to drive wider adoption and prevent billions lost to fraud* (2024) *Consensys.* Available at: https://consensys.io/blog/metamask-reveals-55-surge-in-users-introduces-default-security-alerts-to.

It has become a constantly evolving narrative where traders follow liquidity. There is a feeling now among some that there is just too much going on across too many places to ever be able to keep up with it all and the preferred wisdom is to pick a few routes that you have some conviction in and stick to those, rather than trying to be everywhere across everything.

So, what is the real role of NFT marketplaces, the process for using them and the key considerations?

ROLE OF NFT MARKETPLACES

- **Facilitating transactions:** NFT marketplaces enable the buying, selling and trading of NFTs. They act as intermediaries facilitating these transactions, ensuring they are securely processed using blockchain technology.

- **Visibility for creators:** These platforms provide a venue for artists and creators to showcase their digital art, collectibles or other forms of NFTs to a wider audience.

- **Price discovery:** Marketplaces help in determining the value of NFTs through bidding and sales, aiding in price discovery, which can be quite dynamic due to the unique nature of NFTs.

- **Community building:** Many NFT marketplaces have built-in social features and forums where users can discuss collections, trends and the NFT market, thus fostering a community around NFTs.

Process of buying, selling and trading NFTs

- **Setting up a wallet:** To interact with an NFT marketplace, you first need a digital wallet that supports cryptocurrency, otherwise known as a cryptocurrency wallet. This allows users to store, manage and transact with crypto. It can be a physical device or a software application and serves several essential functions like storage of keys, access to funds and security.

- Wallets contain their own address and your private keys needed to sign cryptocurrency transactions. Never share your private keys with anyone as once access is gained, bad actors can empty your funds with relative ease.

- Most transactions in NFT marketplaces have historically been carried out using Ethereum (ETH), but other cryptocurrencies are also used depending on the platform. These include Solana, Bitcoin, Polygon, Tezos, Avalanche and more.

- **Choosing a marketplace:** Select a marketplace that aligns with your interests. Popular choices include OpenSea, Blur and Magic Eden but there are many more, as referenced earlier in the chapter, each catering to different types of NFTs and communities.

- **Buying NFTs:**

  - Browse the marketplace for NFTs that interest you.

  - Once you find an NFT, you can either buy it at a fixed price or participate in an auction.

  - To complete the purchase, you will need sufficient cryptocurrency in your wallet. The transaction is then recorded on the blockchain. Remember this as the giant diary that keeps a note of every purchase that is made.

- **Selling NFTs:**

  - If you are an artist or NFT owner, you can list your NFT for sale.

  - You can set a fixed price or opt for an auction format.

  - Upon a successful sale, the marketplace typically takes a commission, and the rest of the sale amount is transferred to your wallet. The sale price will be received by you in the cryptocurrency you have listed the NFT for – most likely to be in Ethereum (ETH) but this can then be swapped either for other cryptocurrencies or withdrawn into fiat (£ or $ and so on) using an exchange that allows for withdrawals such as Coinbase, Kraken and Binance.

- **Trading NFTs:**
  - Some marketplaces offer the option to trade NFTs directly with other users.
  - Trading often involves swapping one NFT for another based on mutual agreement on the value of the respective NFTs.
- **Minting NFTs:**
  - Creators can also mint new NFTs on these platforms, which involves creating a new NFT and recording it on the blockchain.
  - This process typically requires paying a gas fee, which can vary based on the blockchain's current demand and congestion. Transactions on blockchain networks (like Ethereum) require these fees, which can fluctuate and have previously been known to be substantial but are rapidly coming down with the 2024 advent of Base by Coinbase, with gas fees being under $1 per transaction, and similarly for Solana too.

Considerations

- **Security:** Ensure that you are using reputable marketplaces such as OpenSea, Magic Eden or Blur and keep your digital wallet secure.
- **Market volatility:** The value of NFTs can be highly volatile, so it is important to do thorough research before investing.

If you are interested in delving deeper into all things cryptocurrency, you should check out another in this BCS series – *Getting Started with Cryptocurrency* – which focuses on just this.[12]

---

12 Baucherel, R. (2024) *Getting started with Cryptocurrency: An introduction to digital assests and blockchain.* BCS.

In summary, NFT marketplaces are critical to the functioning of the NFT ecosystem, offering a platform for the creation, sale, purchase and trading of NFTs. The process involves setting up a digital wallet, choosing a marketplace and then engaging in transactions, keeping in mind the various fees and security considerations.

4 The importance of digital ownership including provenance and authenticity – how it started out in the art world

The concept of digital ownership, especially in the art world, has been fundamentally transformed by the advent of NFTs. NFTs tokenise digital assets, turning them into unique cryptographic tokens that represent various forms of digital content like art, music and videos. This transformation includes creating a digital certificate of authenticity, which ensures the uniqueness and ownership of the digital asset.

One of the key aspects of NFTs in the art world is the concept of provenance. Provenance is essentially a record of ownership of a work of art or an antique, used as a guide to authenticity or quality. It refers to the history of ownership of an item, tracing back through its production, which is crucial in determining the value and authenticity of the piece. This cannot be faked, changed or manipulated in any way.

NFTs address the digital art realm's challenge of ownership and authenticity by providing a transparent and verifiable record of ownership history, ensuring that the digital asset is an original work, not a copy. Such transparency instils trust in the art market, allowing collectors and investors to be confident that the digital asset they are acquiring is genuine.

The value of an NFT can also be significantly influenced by this. Knowing the past owners, the history of transactions and the origins of the NFT can add to its desirability and market value.

It can also reveal the significance of an NFT, such as whether it was created by a renowned artist, part of a significant event or the first of its kind.

Outside of the art market, too, digital ownership via NFTs includes a transparent and immutable record of provenance. This means that the history of the asset, including its creation and all transactions, is permanently recorded on the blockchain. This proof of ownership and history enhances the trust and authenticity of digital assets.

Keen traditional art enthusiasts will note that there were findings to suggest that in March 2024, Damien Hirst had been found to age some of his exhibits artificially so they would seem to have a greater sense of history and provenance. Instead of being produced in the 1990s, as first thought, some pieces were allegedly found to have been made in 2017. This relates to three of the artist's famous works involving dead animals preserved in formaldehyde – a shark, a dove and two calves.[13]

The internet meme 'blockchain solves this' applies here. Because all actions and transactions are public and searchable on the blockchain, they effectively become date stamps and watermarks, therefore the date when a work of art was actually created cannot be faked.

By providing a new revenue stream and a direct connection with their audience, NFTs have empowered digital artists.

This is particularly significant since the ease of replication previously limited the market for digital art. The digital scarcity and provenance established by NFTs solve this problem.

They have introduced new monetisation models for artists through royalties embedded in smart contracts, allowing

---

13 McClenaghan, M. (2024) *Damien Hirst formaldehyde animal works dated to 1990s were made in 2017*, *The Guardian*. Available at: www.theguardian.com/artanddesign/ 2024/mar/19/damien-hirst-formaldehyde-animal-works-dated-to-1990s-were-made-in-2017.

creators to earn a percentage of future sales whenever their NFTs change hands.

One of the big cultural NFT hits of 2021 was the launch in July of that year of 'The Currency' in collaboration with Heni whereby 10,000 unique but almost identical spot paintings were created, each on an A4 sheet of special paper. This number was also chosen to reference the 10,000 unique collectable characters of the CryptoPunks project. They were all handmade by Hirst, initially created in 2016 using enamel paint.

Each artwork was numbered, titled, stamped and signed on the back by the artist with authenticity features on the artwork paper such as a watermark, a microdot and a hologram containing a portrait of the artist, making it difficult to copy or forge, just like a banknote. In doing so, Hirst devised an ingenious system that got people thinking and questioning their sense of worth and value, and whether these pieces of art could be effectively traded, like a currency.

Critically, Hirst mandated that all holders make a choice: they were not able to keep both the physical **and** a digital NFT equivalent that lived on the blockchain, so had to choose one. The one they chose not to keep was then destroyed (either physically in a ceremonial burning at his studio or digitally 'burnt' to be removed from the blockchain).

Each of the physical works were available to purchase for $2,000 during a week-long application window in July 2021. Holders were given one year to decide which out of the physical or the NFT they wanted to keep. The experiment was to discover which format was valued the most by its holders. Would everyone go for the physical piece to hang on their wall or would they go digital and keep the NFT?

This brought up many questions. Will people see it as art they want to keep or an investment in mind – would it be the NFT that appreciates most, or the original piece of artwork signed by Hirst? Which would you prefer to own? And how would you choose? In a video interview with the FT[14] on YouTube, which featured Bank of England governor Mark Carney and Damien Hirst, Hirst said 'Yes, I'm forcing people to make a choice. But the purchaser always has a choice. It is not just "Where's the value?" It is also "Where's the joy?"'

This hybrid offering blurs the lines between art as an asset first and a tradeable commodity second.

How did people choose? To recap, 10,000 were available to be purchased during a one-week application period in July 2021. It ended one year later in July 2022 with 5,149 keeping the physical artwork and 4,851 choosing the NFT, proving that it was hardly a rousing endorsement for the physical form with close to 50 per cent choosing the NFT option. Newport Street Gallery also stated that if the buyers did not exchange their NFT during that period, the physical artwork would be destroyed, while if they chose to exchange it, the NFT would be destroyed.[15]

According to *Whitehot Magazine* in August 2022:

Until the last few hours before the deadline, the NFTs were in the lead – 662 votes against them were cast on the very last day. Was it peer pressure that shifted the balance, causing the eleventh-hour flip in favour of physical paintings? Or was it a visceral recoil against the idea of annihilating unique works of art? [...] Ostensibly, the question posited by 'The Currency' is whether the artworld is driven by financial or aesthetic considerations. However, participants and observers alike seem to be undermining the principle of that question by finding aesthetic pleasure in financial transactions. In postmodernity, everything can be translated into financial terms – personal relationships quite as much as aesthetic

---

14 *Damien Hirst and Mark Carney discuss the artist's new hybrid NFT project 'the currency' (2021) YouTube.* Available at: www.youtube.com/watch?v=SQWrY8E5blU.

15 Designboom (2022) Damien Hirst destroys 1,000 physical artworks of 'the currency' in front of NFT buyers, designboom. Available at: www.designboom.com/art/damien-hirst-destroys-1000-physical-artworks-the-currency-10-13-2022/.

experiences. Advocates of NFTs often refer to themselves as a 'community', not just out of sentiment, but from a hard-headed calculation that a sense of community also has financial value. The purchasers of 'The Currency' create its social value as well as its commercial worth.[16]

Before we switch gears back to the core proponents of digital ownership, it is worth emphasising that the examples of Damien Hirst are fascinating because both strike at the very fabric of digital ownership; firstly, the example of effectively allegedly faking the provenance and heritage of some of his most famous art pieces, and secondly, the real-world experiment of 'The Currency' and seeing if holders valued physical or digital ownership of the NFT version more when given the choice. The result surprised many, with close to 50 per cent choosing the NFT over the physical.

DIGITAL OWNERSHIP RECAP

To recap the most important aspects of digital ownership, below are 10 key areas relating to NFTs, demonstrating why digital ownership is such a cornerstone concept.

1. True ownership

NFTs represent true ownership of digital assets. Unlike traditional digital items, where users only have access or usage rights, NFTs confer actual ownership. This ownership is cryptographically verified on a blockchain, ensuring that the digital asset belongs to the owner in a verifiable and secure manner.

2. Scarcity and exclusivity

Digital ownership through NFTs allows for the creation of scarce and exclusive items in the digital realm. Just like

---

[16] *On Damien Hirst's 'The currency' referendum part two* (no date) *Whitehot Magazine of Contemporary Art.* Available at: https://whitehotmagazine.com/articles/s-currency-referendum-part-two/5495.

physical collectibles or art, NFTs can be limited in quantity, enhancing their value and desirability. Owners can be assured that their digital asset is unique or part of a limited series.

3. Monetisation opportunities

Digital ownership enables creators and owners to monetise their digital assets in various ways. Artists, musicians and other content creators can sell their work directly to their audience as NFTs, earning revenue and royalties. Owners can also resell NFTs on secondary markets, potentially at a profit.

4. Interoperability and portability

NFTs are built on blockchain standards that allow for interoperability across different platforms and ecosystems. Owners can transfer their digital assets between different virtual worlds, marketplaces and applications, providing flexibility and control over their digital possessions.

5. Control and autonomy

With NFTs, owners have complete control over their digital assets. They can decide how to use, display or sell their NFTs without interference from intermediaries or platforms. This autonomy is a significant shift from traditional digital ecosystems where platforms often have substantial control over digital content.

6. Historical and cultural context

The story behind an NFT, including its creation and journey through different owners, can add cultural and historical significance. This narrative can enhance the appeal and cultural value of the NFT, making it more than just a digital asset.

7. Economic and social value

Digital ownership of NFTs can create new economic opportunities and social value. Owners can join communities and participate in events or activities related to their NFTs.

For example, owning a particular NFT might grant access to exclusive content, virtual spaces or community groups, adding layers of value beyond the asset itself.

8. Resellability

For buyers looking to resell NFTs, provenance is crucial in proving the legitimacy and value of the asset. A clear, verified ownership history can facilitate smoother transactions and enhance the resale value of the NFT.

9. Fraud prevention

By maintaining a detailed and transparent record of ownership and transactions, provenance helps prevent fraud. It becomes challenging for malicious actors to create and sell fake NFTs as the true ownership and transaction history are publicly verifiable on the blockchain.

10. Innovation and new business models

NFTs and the concept of digital ownership drive innovation and new business models. They enable decentralised applications (dApps) and services that leverage digital ownership, such as decentralised finance (DeFi), gaming, virtual real estate and more. These innovations expand the possibilities of how digital assets can be used and monetised.

MARKETPLACES, CHALLENGES AND SUMMARY

Outside of these 10 core concepts, the rise of NFTs has also led to the development of decentralised marketplaces, such as OpenSea, Magic Eden, Blur and many more as mentioned in Chapter 3. These platforms leverage blockchain technology and provide a global and inclusive marketplace for digital assets. They allow creators to mint and sell their NFTs directly to buyers, fostering a more direct and equitable market for digital art.

However, this new form of ownership and market for digital art is not without its challenges. Environmental concerns due to the energy consumption of blockchain networks, market saturation and speculative bubbles, as well as copyright and intellectual property issues, are some of the criticisms and challenges that the NFT market faces.

In summary, NFTs have revolutionised the concept of digital ownership in the art world and beyond by ensuring the authenticity and provenance of digital artworks, enhancing value through scarcity, empowering artists with new revenue streams, creating decentralised marketplaces that break down geographical barriers, offering interoperability opportunities and driving innovation in digital ecosystems. Despite the challenges faced, NFTs continue to evolve and have a lasting impact on the art world and beyond.

5 The diverse applications of NFTs beyond art

In years gone by, NFTs were originally perceived as digital art, but as the ecosystem continues to mature in 2024 and beyond, there are many different use cases illustrating its breadth, depth and potential future longevity. We no longer think of it merely as the background technology but what it can actually deliver on the front end too (outside of visuals). Let's dive in!

VIRTUAL PRODUCTS

Virtual products in the form of NFTs represent digital goods that exist solely in the virtual world. These can include digital artwork, virtual clothing for avatars, for example, adidas outfits on Roblox and RTFKT trainers on Fortnite, or items used within video games. The uniqueness of these NFTs lies in their digital scarcity and ownership, making them collectible or usable within certain online platforms or ecosystems.

LVMH, the conglomerate behind some of the biggest brands in fashion, such as Louis Vuitton and Christian Dior, expanded its web3 push by entering into a partnership announced in June 2023 with Epic Games to transform 'their creative pipeline and customer experiences'. The partnership allows LVMH to use 3D creation tools like virtual fitting rooms and fashion shows.

Gucci has made many forays into NFTs and web3 since 2021 and has become one of the most prolific, experimental and innovative global brands in the space. The creation of the Gucci Vault Art Space by Monks envisioned a platform to view and collect the forward-thinking visions of contemporary artists as NFTs. This was followed by personalised PFPs (profile pictures) of the most well-known NFT projects of the time, such as Bored Ape Yacht Club, Cool Cats, World of Women through Gucci Grail, ultra limited edition handmade physical ceramic figures with SUPERGUCCI in collaboration with collectibles brand SUPERPLASTIC, gaming initiatives with Roblox, partnering with Christie's auction house on a generative art collection and allowing payments by crypto in select retail stores.

PHYGITAL

Phygital NFTs bridge the gap between the physical and digital worlds. These NFTs are connected to real-world physical items, ensuring authenticity and ownership. For instance, a luxury bag or watch could be sold along with an NFT, which serves as a certificate of authenticity and ownership history. Allied Analytics has predicted that the global digital clothing market will reach $4.8 billion in 2031, up from approximately $500 million in 2021.

This concept has been increasingly adopted in luxury goods, art and collectibles. Within fashion, Gucci, Louis Vuitton, Balenciaga, RTFKT (Nike) and 9dcc have either created exclusive lines just for their web3 audiences or produced networked products. In the case of 9dcc, a fashion brand built within the web3 space by founder gmoney, who achieved fame helping bring adidas into the metaverse, also creating their own apparel such as hats and t-shirts which have been 'chipped' with NFC or RFID that provides an access gateway into online experiences.

A networked product in fashion is an innovative, digitally interconnected item that leverages blockchain technology and web3 principles to enhance user experience and engagement. As mentioned above, 9dcc is a brand pioneered by renowned NFT collector and influencer gmoney. Their aim is to create a new paradigm in consumer goods by integrating digital assets with physical products. These products are embedded with near-field communication (NFC) chips or QR codes that link to unique digital tokens on the blockchain. The tokens could provide owners with exclusive benefits, authenticate ownership and enable participation in virtual communities or events. By bridging the physical and digital worlds, such a product not only offers tangible utility but also fosters a sense of belonging and engagement within a broader decentralised network.

One nascent upstart making waves in recent times is MNTGE, founded by Nick Adler and Brennan Russo. They launched the vintage clothing brand in 2022, which integrates blockchain technology into garments. Nick Adler had this to say, posted on X (formerly Twitter) to CNBC in March 2024:

The first and foremost thing we've done is integrate NFC chips into our products. Super simple, no logins, you tap your phone up against it, tap the link that comes up which shows the verified digital receipt (token) of the physical item. This will be able to tell anyone who taps it, who designed the item, what number it is in the collection, what potential rips and tears the clothing has (traits), potentially who wore the item e.g. if it was previously worn by a celebrity.[17]

In September 2023, a startup called IYK, founded by Ryan Ouyang and Christopher Lee, raised $16.8 million, led by tech investment giants A16Z. Their overall premise is to 'create tangible digital experiences'. In practice, this provides a physical goods brand with the opportunity to 'chip' any item, create a digital twin and introduce new layers of engagement and access in doing so. 'By combining web3 and NFC [near field communication] chip technology, the IYK Platform enables every brand on the planet to deliver novel consumer experiences', Arianna Simpson, a general partner at A16Z crypto, said in a statement.

Their popularity spans fashion, events, music and art – all very experiential, tactile and sensory verticals where the in-person experience is key. They have worked with the likes of adidas, 9dcc, Doodles, Mastercard, Johnny Walker, Atlantic Records, Art Blocks and more since their inception.

---

[17] MNTGE (2024) [X] 28 March. Available at: https://x.com/mntge_io/status/1773420468357517439.

LOYALTY

Loyalty NFTs are used in customer loyalty programmes. Instead of traditional points or cards, businesses can offer NFTs that provide unique experiences, discounts or access to products. These NFTs can increase customer engagement by offering more personalised and exclusive rewards than traditional loyalty programmes.

Starbucks trialled the Odyssey programme exclusively in the USA, which was built on the Polygon blockchain and allowed people to buy, collect and trade Starbucks-specific NFTs. In March 2024, they announced that the Odyssey beta was being sunset and their next moves were still unannounced at the time of going to print. Notably, Starbucks received a $4 million grant in 2022 from Polygon to build up the loyalty programme on the blockchain, so there is an expectation that it will continue but in a different guise than as seen currently with Odyssey.

KITH, the cultural icon in streetwear and hype culture, created the KITH Friends programme, which started out with the NFT project Invisible Friends. Together they created an entire line of apparel featuring both brands, including hats, jackets, tees and customised trainers only for holders of three different KITH Friends NFTs. The size of the NFT (M, L and XL) corresponded to which 'fit' they liked the most.

They had this to say about the initiative on launch:

> *Designed in partnership with Invisible Friends, we've created an experience that bridges digital and physical spaces through a collection of special non-fungible tokens that grant holders unique and exclusive access to upcoming Kith launches. Each Kith Friend™ debuts looks from our upcoming Summer 2022 collection. Holders of these NFTs will be given all the physical products their Kith Friend™ is wearing.*[18]

---

18 *Kith for Invisible Friends Collection* (no date) *Kith.* Available at: https://kith.com/collections/kith-for-invisible-friends-collection.

Monks created a collaborative digital downloadable report on web3 loyalty with Reddit, Salesforce and Polygon, delving deep into this topic, how brands can utilise it and what they can do to involve the community. Litman said:

> *These use cases essentially create community-driven programs that deliver business value and benefit [...] We're not talking about just community for the sake of people being part of something; there is generally business outcome and goals tied to that community driving aspect.*[19]

In the article on Monks.com 'Decoding web3: How Blockchain is Transforming Commerce and Brands', Xuanmai Vo discusses the role of web3 in facilitating community building, Litman highlights what he refers to as 'the four C's': creativity, culture, community and commerce. Emphasising the significance of relationships in branding, he states, 'In web3, this dynamic relationship between the brand and the consumer transforms into a more robust, two-way relationship, where consumers actively engage, creating a reciprocal exchange.'[20] The transparency provided by blockchain technology thus enhances the connection between brands and consumers.

Dom Pérignon recognised this potential when it partnered with Monks to create an exclusive web3 marketplace, inspired by its collaboration with Lady Gaga. This move significantly enhanced the brand's cultural relevance. The immersive web platform featured 100 NFTs representing the Dom Pérignon Vintage 2010 and Dom Pérignon Rosé Vintage 2006 collections. Each NFT purchase included a physical bottle of the corresponding wine. By linking the NFT to the physical bottle, Dom Pérignon generated an additional revenue stream and offered consumers digital collectibles that could be traded on the secondary market, where their value increased by nearly 1,500 per cent. This shoppable experience successfully

---

19 *Decoding web3: How blockchain is Transforming Commerce and brands* (no date) *Media.Monks.* Available at: https://media.monks.com/articles/decoding-web3-how-blockchain-transforming-commerce-and-brands.

20 Ibid.

bridged the virtual and real worlds, positioning Dom Pérignon as a pioneer in the web3 space.

The renowned jewellery brand Tiffany and Co. capitalised on the web3 trend early by engaging the CryptoPunks community, creating a tokenised reward specifically for them. The NFTs, ingeniously dubbed NFTiffs, were made available to 250 holders only, who could collect these unique digital assets and exchange them for customisable gold pendants. Tiffany and Co. set a precedent by merging fine jewellery with the digital world, achieving remarkable success as NFTiffs sold out in just 20 minutes at a mint price of 30 ETH, generating an impressive $12.5 million in revenue.

Macy's has excelled in creating spaces for multi-user, communal interaction with their brand at the forefront. In collaboration with Monks, the department store virtualised its iconic Thanksgiving Day Parade in 2022. This included a virtual Sixth Avenue featuring parade balloons inspired by popular web3 communities at the time such as Cool Cats, Boss Beauties, VeeFriends and more. Visitors could enjoy the parade and enter virtual storefronts to purchase digital collectibles, with proceeds benefiting NYC charity, Big Brothers Big Sisters of America. These collectibles could also be resold on web3 platforms like OpenSea. Macy's innovative approach demonstrates how web3 capabilities can foster new shoppable, social experiences, introducing an entirely new product category for the retailer.

HUGO BOSS made waves in May 2024 by launching HUGO BOSS XP, an 'innovative loyalty program that introduces a new world of engagement'.

It has been billed as a:

> *pioneering omnichannel member experience that is centered around the HUGO BOSS customer app. The program lever-ages the latest technologies as part of an ambitious multi-year roadmap to set a new industry benchmark for customer engagement, focusing on member experience and customer*

lifetime value. In doing so, HUGO BOSS is making another important investment into the company's future.[21]

The release announcement continues:

It seamlessly blends traditional loyalty features, such as levels and points, with innovative blockchain-supported elements. The program incorporates initial Web3 features to open new customer engagement opportunities: Members can collect and redeem tokens (NFTs) through their purchases and other interactions across channels and brands. They act as keys to unlock exclusive products, unique brand experiences, and further offers from BOSS and HUGO or sponsorship and cooperation partners. Part of the plan is the future possibility for customers to trade tokens. The new program strengthens HUGO BOSS' position as an industry innovator. [...] With our new membership program, we are taking customer engagement to a new level, further enhancing, and expanding interactions with our brands. By deepening the relationship with our customers, we are driving a higher lifetime value thereby further advancing with our profitable growth journey.[22]

The first version of the new membership programme initially launched in the UK in June 2024. The current customer loyalty programme, HUGO BOSS EXPERIENCE, will be fully upgraded by the introduction of HUGO BOSS XP over the next few years with further countries to follow. Existing members will be seamlessly transferred to the new programme.

Oliver Timm concludes in a LinkedIn post:

By leveraging data and emerging technologies – such as blockchain, Web3 or NFTs – we are creating an entirely new

---

21 Ag, H.B. (2024) *Hugo boss launches innovative customer loyalty program and introduces a new world of engagement, HUGO BOSS Group: Home.* Available at: https://group.hugoboss.com/en/newsroom/news/news-detail/hugo-boss-launches-innovative-customer-loyalty-program-and-introduces-a-new-world-of-engagement.

22 Ibid.

platform that offers hyper-personalized, perfectly meshed omnichannel experiences, which will also take local customer preferences into account. I am convinced that this next level loyalty program will enable us to further unlock the full poten-tial of our brands with meaningful digital interactions and deepen our relationship with our customers worldwide. It is also an important milestone in our journey of becoming the leading, premium tech-driven fashion platform worldwide.[23]

PFPs

Profile picture project (PFP) NFTs are primarily used on social media platforms like X, Discord, WhatsApp, Telegram and many more. At their core, a PFP NFT is a digital token or artwork designed to be displayed as a person's social media profile picture. Many of the world's most popular NFT collections are PFPs. The most notable during this period in time and history are CryptoPunks (released in June 2017 with a 10,000 supply) and Bored Apes (released in April 2021, also with a 10,000 supply). They gained most of their initial popularity as a form of digital identity and a status symbol or flex. There is also a tribal and community aspect of owning a particular project PFP, akin to being a member of a private club.

PFPs effectively live at the intersection of collectibles and generative art. They are collectibles in that they usually come in large quantities, for example, 2–10,000, and have varying degrees of rarity, similar to trading cards. A 'floor' PFP is known to be the lowest entry point into the project and a 'grail' is the rarest and therefore has a higher entry purchase price. Each will have different traits and some people like to find one that they think looks like them or has elements of familiarity. If it does bear a visual resemblance to you in the real world, some are known to recognise people's PFPs on their social profiles like Twitter (X) and Discord, and if and when it gets changed, it can be a big 'moment' on newsfeeds.

23 Timm, O. (2024) *Oliver Timm on LinkedIn*. Available at: www.linkedin.com/posts/ oliver-timm-59043247_we-are-taking-a-bold-step-forward-in-customer-activity-7198962227087818753-WXSN/?utm_source=share&utm_medium=member_ios

There are numerous other collections vying for the real estate of consumers' social profile pictures that were of the moment at the time, including Meebits, Mutant Apes, Pudgy Penguins, Cool Cats, Azuki, Doodles, Clone X, Moonbirds, Invisible Friends, Deadfellaz, Adam Bomb Squad, Mfers, Milady, Psychedelics Anonymous, Sappy Seals and many more.

Female founder-led projects such as World of Women and Boss Beauties also provided support, mentoring, community and encouraged greater female participation within this nascent space. These NFTs granted access to exclusive communities, events and token gated commerce opportunities like merch and physical collectibles along with being a 'flex' offering a sense of IYKYK (if you know, you know).

Doxxing is the notion of revealing someone's identity or personal details that they have chosen not to be made public. Doxxing someone against their will is seen as an unacceptable invasion of privacy. One of the most high-profile examples was when Buzzfeed chose to reveal the identity of Wylie Aronow and Greg Solano, co-founders of Yuga Labs and famously of the Bored Ape Yacht Club. This is because PFPs can be also a pseudonymous identity for some, whereby you do not know what they actually look like in the real world and only know them online by their profile picture. This may be because they do not want to be 'doxxed' and choose to have an online persona, such as Gordon Goner and Garga, founders of Yuga Labs.

Other examples include gmoney (a well-known influencer and founder of 9dcc) and Betty from Deadfellaz, who both themselves chose to doxx their own identities instead of being a CryptoPunk PFP in gmoney's case and a Deadfellaz in Betty's case. Both at the time were seen as big cultural moments and a positive step forward for their further legitimacy.

GENERATIVE ART + DIGITAL ART + FINE ART

Generative art NFTs are created using algorithms, often incorporating AI, to produce unique artworks. Digital art NFTs encompass various digital creations, while fine art NFTs are digital representations or tokens of physical fine art.

These NFTs democratise art ownership and create new avenues for artists to monetise their work. Beeple kicked off this new wave, going from being a relative unknown to a now world-famous star. NFTs have created entirely new artists or propelled more traditionally known artists to new heights. Refik Anadol, Tyler Hobbs, Snowfro, Sam Spratt, Vinnie Hager, Seerlight, Grant Yun, Dmitri Cherniak, Matt DesLauriers, Corey Van Lew were all probably unknown to many before NFTs.

Some of these digitally native artists have even found themselves accepted by traditional auction houses like Sotheby's and Christie's, which have exhibited their work to a more traditional art-buying audience. Traditional fine artists like Murakami and Damien Hirst have also found great success with NFTs through projects such as RTFKT, CloneX and The Currency (as seen further in Chapter 4).

MUSIC

Music NFTs represent ownership or partial ownership of a musical work. Artists use them to sell their music directly to fans, providing a new revenue stream and closer artist–fan relationships. These NFTs can include songs, albums or exclusive content like behind-the-scenes material.

In March 2021, Kings of Leon released their new album, *When You See Yourself*, in the form of an NFT and became the first band ever to do so.[24] The band released this as three types of tokens.

The first type comprises a special album package, the second is a live show package with front row seats for life, and the third offers a special audiovisual package.

---

[24] Hissong, S. (2021) *Kings of Leon will be the first band to release an album as an NFT, Rolling Stone.* Available at: www.rollingstone.com/pro/news/kings-of-leon-when-you-see-yourself-album-nft-crypto-1135192/.

Over $2 million of tokens were sold. The three types of tokens include artwork from Night After Night, the band's longstanding creative partner; YellowHeart, a company that uses blockchain technology to provide better direct-to-fan relationships by bringing value back to music, developed the smart contracts and intelligence inside each token.

YellowHeart minted 18 unique-looking 'golden tickets' as part of the Kings of Leon NFT release. The band auctioned six of the 18 pieces and vaulted the remaining 12, as a painter does with a series of art.

'Each one of those is a unique NFT with the most incredible Kings of Leon art you've ever seen',[25] explains Katz.

Each 'golden ticket' also unlocks an actual concert ticket – marking the first time a music ticket has been sold officially as an NFT. Whoever owns the token is guaranteed four front-row seats to any Kings of Leon concert during each tour for life. The token owner also gets a VIP experience that includes a personal driver, a concierge at the show to take care of their needs, a hangout with the band before the show and exclusive lounge access. Upon leaving the show, the fan's car will have four bags filled with every item from the merch booth.

The album was released through the usual channels, but the NFT version available on YellowHeart was the only product offering special perks.

As part of the $50 token, owners receive enhanced media, such as an alternative, moving album cover, a digital download of the music and a limited-edition vinyl version.

The sale of the album was open for two weeks. After that time, no more were made, and the NFT became a tradable collectible. Katz told the *Rolling Stone* in 2021,

> *Over the last 20 years – two lost decades – we've seen the devaluation of music. Music has become great at selling*

---

25 Ibid.

everything except music. There's been a race to the bottom where, for as little money as possible, you have access to all of it. Previously, it cost $20 to go get one song.[26]

Before Kings of Leon's release, NFTs were a relatively underground following in music made up largely of DJs and producers with many musicians seeking out additional revenue streams in the concertless era of the pandemic. The likes of Maroon 5, Zhu, The Man, Shawn Mendes, Grimes, Avenged Sevenfold, deadmau5, 3LAU, Linkin Park's Mike Shinoda, among others, have all jumped on since.

Shinoda notably released ZIGGURATS in December 2021, the first generative NFT mixtape. It was a collection of 5,000 unique audio and visual NFTs that were created from new artwork and music by Mike Shinoda. No two items were the same visually and musically, but some are rarer. It sold out within minutes of being available. 'I've described it to some people as a "song that's not a song". But it is also an EP that's not an EP, an NFT that's not an NFT, and an art project that's more than just a picture.'[27]

YellowHeart was founded by Josh Katz in 2018 and at the time, was billed as sitting at the intersection of what has happened to crypto-currency and what is about to happen to art and tickets. Items that once traded on the street for currency now trade across unique digital platforms in return for digital currency.

YellowHeart is harnessing the blockchain's potential to revolutionise ticket and art sales, establishing a new asset class that ensures buyers can trace the provenance of tradeable items irrevocably. This system also guarantees that creators receive a portion of all future profits generated from trading their work.

---

26 Hissong, S. (2021) *Kings of Leon will be the first band to release an album as an NFT*, *Rolling Stone*. Available at: www.rollingstone.com/pro/news/kings-of-leon-when-you-see-yourself-album-nft-crypto-1135192/.

27 Shutler, A. (2021) Mike Shinoda teases new 'Generative mixtape' "ziggurats", NME. Available at: www.nme.com/news/music/mike-shinoda-teases-new-generative-mixtape-ziggurats-3103035.

SPORTS COLLECTIBLES

Sports collectible NFTs digitise traditional sports memorabilia, such as trading cards or videos of memorable sports moments. They provide fans with a new way to connect with their favourite teams and athletes, often including interactive elements or exclusive content. The most notable example of this is NBA Top Shot.

NBA Top Shot is a digital collectibles platform developed by Dapper Labs in collaboration with the National Basketball Association (NBA) and the NBA Players Association. Launched in 2020, it allows users to buy, sell and trade officially licensed NBA collectible highlights called 'Moments'. These Moments are essentially short video clips of memorable plays from NBA games, each backed by blockchain technology to ensure their authenticity and scarcity. In May 2022, it surpassed $1 billion in total sales.[28] In its early phase, it experienced rapid growth. In February 2021 alone, the platform recorded sales of $224 million, marking a peak during the initial NFT boom. Comparatively, in February 2022, sales revenue was reported at $47.5 million.[29]

Key aspects of NBA Top Shot included:

Blockchain technology: NBA Top Shot operates on the Flow blockchain, which was also developed by Dapper Labs. This technology ensures that each Moment is unique, verifiable and cannot be duplicated, providing a sense of digital ownership similar to physical trading cards.

Moments: Moments are the core of NBA Top Shot. They feature video highlights of specific plays, such as a spectacular dunk, a game-winning shot or an incredible assist. Each Moment is associated with a particular player and game, and they

---

28 Perez, A.J. (2022) *NBA top shot reaches $1B in sales amid NFT market downturn, Front Office Sports.* Available at: https://frontofficesports.com/nba-top-shot-reaches-1b-in-sales-amid-nft-market-downturn/.

29 Minter, R. (2022) *NBA top shot sales revenue fell by more than $10 million in February, BeInCrypto.* Available at: https://beincrypto.com/nba-top-shot-sales-revenue-fell-10-million-february/.

come in various levels of rarity: Common, Rare, Legendary and Ultimate.

Packs: Similar to traditional trading cards, NBA Top Shot Moments are sold in packs. These packs are released periodically and contain a random assortment of Moments. The excitement of opening a pack and discovering which Moments are inside contributes to the appeal of the platform.

Marketplace: NBA Top Shot includes a marketplace where users can buy and sell individual Moments. Prices can vary widely based on factors like the player's popularity, the significance of the play and the rarity of the Moment. Some Moments have sold for thousands of dollars, especially those featuring superstar players or historic plays.

Challenges and collecting: NBA Top Shot also incorporates challenges and collecting incentives. Users can complete specific collections or sets of Moments to earn rewards, such as exclusive Moments or other bonuses.

Community and engagement: NBA Top Shot has built a strong community of collectors and fans who engage through various online platforms. Integrating social elements, such as showcasing collections and discussing trades, has further fuelled interest in the platform.

To conclude, NBA Top Shot combined the excitement of sports fandom with the emerging technology of digital collectibles, creating a unique and engaging experience for basketball fans and collectors alike.

FASHION

Fashion NFTs are digital representations of clothing and accessories, often used in virtual worlds or as part of phygital products. Designers and brands like Gucci, adidas, Dolce & Gabbana, Hugo Boss, Louis Vuitton and many more use them to explore new forms of expression, deepen loyalty and create new customer engagement opportunities in the digital realm.

GAMING AND IN-GAME ITEMS

Gaming NFTs transform in-game items like weapons, skins or characters into tradeable assets, providing players with ownership and the potential for real-world value. They are a key element in play-to-earn gaming models.

UTILITY AND MEMBERSHIP

Utility NFTs offer practical benefits, such as access to services, exclusive content or membership privileges. They are used in various industries to provide customers with value beyond mere ownership, like access to events or clubs. (See loyalty for brand examples.)

VIRTUAL REAL ESTATE

Virtual real estate NFTs represent ownership of land or property in virtual worlds. These NFTs can be developed, traded or used to host digital experiences, playing a significant role in the growing metaverse.

FRACTIONAL

Fractional NFTs divide ownership of a high-value NFT into smaller, more affordable parts. This allows multiple individuals to own a share of a single NFT, making high-value assets more accessible.

RENTALS

Rental NFTs enable the temporary use of digital assets through smart contracts. Users can access and utilise an NFT for a limited period, offering flexibility and affordability.

COLLATERISED

Collateralised NFTs are used as collateral in decentralised finance (DeFi) applications. Owners can borrow funds against their NFTs, unlocking liquidity while retaining ownership of their digital assets.

Each of these NFT types offers unique opportunities and challenges, reflecting the diverse and evolving nature of the NFT market.

In summary, there are 15 different types of NFTs as referenced in this chapter. You now know everything from what and how to use a collateralised NFT, to what is fractionalising (breaking down into small bites) to fashion, gaming, loyalty, sports and generative AI.

There is a wide gamut of variations and use cases for NFTs over and above art and PFPs, which came to the fore from 2021 to 2023.

Loyalty NFTs will gain more prominence in years to come, I believe, as brand loyalty programmes become increasingly more blockchain-enthused, as we are seeing with Hugo Boss in 2024. Fractional NFTs will also grow in usage as they provide users with the ability to collectively own a piece of a high-value NFT rather than individually owning the full entity outright.

Sports, fashion and music will see new usage opportunities, providing access to communities or will provide the ability to purchase low-supply items such as clothing, tickets or music and merch.

6   NFTs as cultural capital, identity, status and the new flex

NFTs have emerged since early 2021 as a significant force in the realms of culture, identity, status and 'flex', or show of wealth and success, for several reasons. During my time deeply entrenched within the space, I became fascinated by the notion of cultural capital. Why?

NFTs, along with being attention tokens that need ongoing momentum, have become an influential form of cultural capital in the digital age.

Pierre Bourdieu was a French sociologist who wrote extensively on power and social relationships. Bourdieu studied under Marxist philosophers, and he believed that ownership of economic capital was the root of power. However, he theorised that there were three types of capital: economic, cultural and social. He considered cultural and social capital to be 'disguised forms of economic capital'. Cultural and social capital refer to the non-financial social assets that promote social mobility beyond economic means. These assets include education, intellect, style of speech, dress or physical appearance, but in the context of NFTs, they extend to digital ownership and identity.[30]

For example, unconscious bias is gained from the following without us even realising: attending a prestigious university,

---

30 Ramsey, G. (2024) *Cultural capital theory of Pierre Bourdieu, Simply Psychology.* Available at: www.simplypsychology.org/cultural-capital-theory-of-pierre-bourdieu.html.

having a high-profile job, an expensive watch or car, an art collection featuring originals from popular names or owning a rare trainer, vintage bag or a piece of furniture from a well-known designer. These are all examples that provide cultural and societal advantages that appear to be unrelated to the economic capital required to pay for them. It is knowledge capital, an in-the-know 'flex'. It is signalling who you are and what interests you. This all illustrates that social and cultural capital have similar power structures to economic capital. Ever heard the term 'all money and no sense'? That is a poor use of economic capital!

Let's delve a little deeper into these three types of cultural capital.

CULTURAL CAPITAL IN AN EMBODIED STATE

This form of cultural capital is the knowledge, skills and tastes that you acquire as a result of your standing in society. In particular, it is the knowledge that allows people to maintain their social standing by conforming to cultural expectations. For example, being in the know about generative artists and knowing your Jack Butcher from your Refik Anadol is in itself an embodied state of cultural capital.

Bourdieu theorised that this form of cultural capital was picked up almost unconsciously by individuals as they absorb the behaviours of their friends and peers, to the point that social advantages like the people you know within the industry and which events you attend to meet your peers become ingrained into your personality, into who you are.

Cultural capital in an embodied state is closely related to the idea of a habitus – a concept coined by Bourdieu that was very important to his philosophy. Bourdieu described the habitus as an unconscious 'feel for the game', a sense of what you should or should not do in social situations, a sense of where you fit into the social 'game', and a sense of how to win at that game.

This unconscious and largely invisible nature of embodied cultural capital would make it appear far removed from economic capital. However, embodied cultural capital is acquired by being raised around these kinds of behaviours – and the kinds of behaviours you are exposed to are directly correlated to the economic silo in which you exist. Further, this 'sense of the game' can be essential in moving up the social ladder and gaining access to wealth.

CULTURAL CAPITAL IN AN OBJECTIFIED STATE

This form of capital is, put simply, the objectification of capital. This means the physical objects that can be owned, such as books, pieces of art or historical artefacts that convey your sense of identity and self. They confer cultural knowledge and prestige whereby these objects all have cultural or symbolic significance and will typically communicate something about the owner's social standing. For example, a wealthy person with an extensive collection of rare books, cars or watches is able to project a sense of intellectuality, success and competence about themselves by owning these objects.

Cultural capital in an objectified state also requires some level of cultural understanding in order to be interpreted or understood. In theory, the cultural artefacts in museums are available to everyone, but it requires a certain level of educational context for someone to truly understand the piece of art that they are looking at and get the most out of it. In fact, Bourdieu found empirically that the amount of time that people spent in a museum of art correlated directly to how much education they had attained. Those who had had more schooling spent more time in the museum.

Bourdieu also discussed machines as objectified cultural capital. One must have a certain level of knowledge – embodied cultural capital – in order to operate the machine and therefore gain the economic capital that one is rewarded with their ability to operate the machine. Objects like these that require embodied cultural capital in order for them to be useful or meaningful to the person interacting with it were considered by Bourdieu to be cultural capital in an objectified state.

CULTURAL CAPITAL IN AN INSTITUTIONALISED STATE

Institutionalised cultural capital is a formal recognition from an institution that a person has some intellectual asset. This is usually in the form of a degree or certification credential. This form of social capital allows the person who has it to directly transfer their cultural capital into actual economic assets. It allows individuals with a degree to access higher-paying jobs and more elite professional and social circles than they would otherwise have had access to. For example, just because you went to a great university and got good grades does not instantly guarantee a job at the end of it. It does, however, offer greater chances of opportunities through a network effect and also offers additional pathways into future employment.

Other ways of expressing these traits include the following.

Digital ownership and identity

NFTs represent a unique form of digital ownership that can be directly associated with an individual's online identity. Owning certain NFTs – especially those that are rare or created by renowned artists – can be a status symbol, signalling a person's taste, passions, interests, wealth and technological savviness.

This form of digital ownership is becoming increasingly important in online and virtual spaces. The unique and non-fungible nature of these digital assets makes them valuable not only as investments but also as tools for personal expression and identity formation. They allow individuals to showcase who they are and what they value in a digitally native format.

Cultural value creation

NFTs represent a paradigm shift in how cultural value is created and perceived. They offer a new way for creators and originators of culture to participate directly in the rewards of platforms that host their work. This is particularly impactful in scenarios where creators traditionally received little to no financial benefit despite contributing significantly to a platform's cultural and economic value. NFTs provide a mechanism for creators to monetise their work and engage directly with their audience.

Community building and engagement

NFTs are also playing a pivotal role in community building. They enable direct and transparent interactions between creators and collectors, fostering new dynamics in the digital space. By eliminating intermediaries like galleries or record labels, NFTs empower creators to have more control over their work and its distribution. This shift is particularly significant in the context of web3, where decentralisation and direct engagement are key elements.

Representation and empowerment

NFTs are being used by various cultural and minority groups to represent their identities and narratives in the digital world. There is the Squiggle DAO, Meebits DAO, Nouns DAO and the Apecoin DAO, for example, which are all centred around their specific projects. This aspect of NFTs has been particularly empowering for communities, allowing them to create a deeper tribalistic connection with like-minded people of shared interests and hobbies.

Status symbol and 'new flex'

NFTs have become a new form of status symbol, akin to luxury goods or high-end collectibles in the physical world. Owning rare or highly sought-after NFTs, especially those created by renowned artists or tied to popular cultural phenomena, can signify wealth, technological savviness and a cutting-edge approach to collecting and investment. This aspect has made NFTs a 'new flex' for the digital age, where displaying one's digital assets is a way to showcase success and sophistication in a rapidly evolving digital culture.

In summary, NFTs, ultimately, as cultural capital, represent a significant shift in how cultural value, identity and status are perceived and manifested in the digital world. They provide a new platform for artistic expression, community building and personal branding while also serving as a modern status symbol in an increasingly digital world. They are reshaping the landscape of art, collectibles and cultural expression, making it more inclusive, diverse and accessible to various communities and individuals.

7   The leaders of the space

In this chapter, we are going to first champion the individuals, the artists, the collectors, the leaders, the influencers, the companies and projects who have all collectively been an active part of, shaped and driven forward the ecosystem from 2021 to 2024. Throughout this time of being deeply immersed within the space, I have met many incredible visionaries who strongly believe that crypto has the power to truly transform industries and lives.

We have also selected three brand case studies to go into greater detail about what they did, how they did it and what impact they made. We selected adidas, Oracle Red Bull Racing and the Australian Tennis Open. I hope you enjoy and learn some new things from each of the brands about how they found new audiences, created new experiences and harnessed web3 technologies.

Let's start with the lists below, being a small cross-section of all the amazing people, companies and projects.

ARTISTS

Refik Anadol, Beeple, Bobby Hundreds, ThankYouX, Betty from Deadfellaz, Jack Butcher, Matt Hall, John Watkinson, gmoney, Tyler Hobbs, XCOPY, Dmitri Cherniak, Kjetil Golid,

Seerlight, Claire Silver, Terrell Jones, Mad Dog Jones, Cory Van Lew, Grant Yun, FVCKRENDER, DeeKay, Matt DesLauriers, Robert Alice, DEFACED, Matt Kane, Takashi Murakami, Dave Krugman, Bryan Brinkman, Spottie Wifi, Sam Spratt, Orkhan, Zach Lieberman, Vinnie Hager, Justin Aversano, Lascaux, Des Lucrece, Devon DeJardin, zancan, Matt Kane, William Mapan, Ovie Farukh (OSF), Clon, WARHODL, Tom Sachs

NOTABLE COLLECTORS AND COMPANY FIGUREHEADS

J1mmy.eth, Nate Alex, Kai Turner, Pranksy, Erick Calderon (Snowfro), Sillytuna, Seedphrase, Punk6529, Jamie Burke, Richerd, Chris Dixon, Chris Maddern, Fonz, Julian Holguin, Luca Netz, Alexis Ohanian, Frank DeGods, Wylie Aronow, Greg Solano, Ingi Erlingsson, Farokh Sarmad, Michael Figge, Adriana Hoppenbrouwer-Pereira, Marco Marchesi, David Horvarth, Ian Rogers, Pascal Gauthier, Ariel Wengroff, Micael Barilaro, Simon Squibb, Michael Bouhanna, Roger Dickerman, Keith Grossman, Ryan Ouyang, Christopher Lee

NOTABLE INFLUENCERS AND PEOPLE OF INTEREST

Sam (Stats), Julie Allen, Adam Crowle, Daniel Mitchell, Michael Anderson (Mando), Chana Kanzen, Quinn and Jonathon Button, Deeze, Brian Trunzo, Max Comparetto, Mathew Sweezey, Sebastian Oddo, Grateful Ape, Beast, Lucas Verra, Winny, Amanda Cassatt, Jennifer Roebuck, Andre da Costa, Wale, S4mmy, Bcheque, Legendary, Evan Luza, Steve Aoki (top signal), Morgan Evans, Kevin Ma, Dan Lewis, Ben Lunt, Franklin, Machi, Harold, Stacey, Vlad, Tareq, Ben and Erika from adidas, Tim Walther, Simon Clowes, Tony Herrera, Dan Podasca, Omri Bouton, Nizzar Ben Chekroune, Aventurine, Aleskandra Art, Sebastian Oddo

NOTABLE COMPANIES FROM 2021 TO 2024

Art Blocks, Larva Labs, Yuga Labs, Ledger, adidas, Nike, RTFKT, Rug Radio, Porsche, McLaren, Salesforce, Reddit, Polygon,

Rainbow, MetaMask, Coinbase, Phantom, Monks, Macy's, Gucci, A16Z, Solana, OpenSea, ENS, The Nifty, Mocaverse, Dune, Nansen, REKT, CoinDesk, Metaversal, Hypemoon by Hypebeast, 9dcc, Tokenproof, Lucky Trader, Shopify, DRESSX, This Outfit Does Not Exist, The Fabricant, Americana, ARIANEE, Fortnite, Starbucks, Lacoste, Puma, Porsche, Lamborghini, Fiat, MoonPay, MNTGE, MMERCH, Christie's, Sotheby's, Mastercard, PUMA, Magic Wallet, Oracle Red Bull Racing

NOTABLE PROJECTS FROM 2021 TO 2024

CryptoPunks, Fidenza, Pudgy Penguins, Grifters by XCOPY, Gazers by Matt Kane, Chromie Squiggle by Snowfro, Azuki, Meridian by Matt DesLauriers, Winds of Yawanawa by Refik Anadol, Creepz, Mutant Ape Yacht Club, PROOF Collective, Moonbirds, Otherside by Yuga Labs, Quirkies, Sappy Seals, Admit One and 9dcc by gmoney, Rektguy, Bored Ape Kennel Club, Checks and Opepen by Jack Butcher, Mocaverse, Letters by Vinnie Hager, adidas Into the Metaverse, World of Women, Boss Beauties, Cool Cats, RTFKT, Invisible Friends, Doodles, SupDucks, VeeFriends, Smilesss, Bored Ape Yacht Club, Mutant Apes, DeGods, Clone X, Meebits, Deadfellaz, Dour Darcels, Robotos, Damien Hirst The Currency, ArtBall by Australian Tennis Open, Porsche NFT, McLaren NFT, Fiat NFT, Kings of Leon NFT album, Adam Bomb Squad, Lacoste UND3, Gucci Vault, SUPERGUCCI, Nakamigos Mfers, CyberBrokers, 10KTF Gucci Grail, Circle of Frens by Chikai, Poolsuite, MNTGE Pass, KITH Friends, Pepe, Wif, Mad Lads, Node Monkes, WAGMI United, Oracle Red Bull Racing: Velocity Pass

CASE STUDY 1 – ORACLE RED BULL RACING: VELOCITY PASS

Oracle Red Bull Racing (ORBR) introduced the Velocity Pass back in 2023 and returned again in 2024 with Series 2.0.[31] The

---

[31] *Velocity series presents: Velocity Pass 2.0* (no date) *Buy & Sell Bitcoin, Ether*. Available at: www.bybit.com/en/promo/nft-events/velocity-pass-V2.

Velocity Pass is billed as a front-row access into this unique series of digital art and was a limited edition of only 1,000 for 2023 and 2,000 for 2024.[32] The pass itself is a dynamic work of art that evolves over the course of the Formula 1 race season to reflect key moments.

In partnership with Bybit and curated in collaboration with AOI, it created a foundation for emerging art and technology. The 2023 series consisted of four releases coinciding with the Dutch, Japan, United States and Abu Dhabi races throughout the 2023 season. Each release featured a range of NFT collections, including publicly available open-edition and limited-edition NFTs exclusively accessible to holders of the Velocity Pass. Season 1 proved to be a huge commercial and cultural success, with artwork from names such as Snowfro and Jack Butcher reaching highs of 5.99 and 4.99 ETH respectively. Other artists included Rik Oostenbroek and Per Kristian Stoveland.

In addition to the high floor price sales, the artist drops played an important role in expanding their collector bases, ultimately reaching new audiences, attracting fresh interest and enthusiasm to the world of digital collectibles. Incredibly, 92 per cent of collectors for Erick Snowfro's /// collection were totally new to his work, highlighting the series' ability to engage audiences beyond traditional boundaries. Oliver Hughes, Chief Marketing Officer at Oracle Red Bull Racing, in a launch announcement, April 2024, said:

The Velocity Pass allows fans to own a piece of the team's legacy, reimagined through the lens of talented digital artists. After the fantastic response in 2023 to the collaboration with Bybit, we're looking forward to connecting with our passionate fanbase in a new and exciting way once again.[33]

---

32 Bybit (2024) *Bybit and Oracle Red Bull racing ignite excitement with Velocity Series 2.0: Unveiling innovative divisible, data-driven ART NFTS, PR Newswire: news distribution, targeting and monitoring.* Available at: www.prnewswire.com/in/news-releases/bybit-and-oracle-red-bull-racing-ignite-excitement-with-velocity-series-2-0-unveiling-innovative-divisible-data-driven-art-nfts-302112681.html.

33 Ibid.

Season 2 of the Velocity Pass is billed as a groundbreaking web3 collaboration between Bybit, Oracle Red Bull Racing, Art On The Internet and world-renowned digital artists who will create digital art collections inspired by race team data.

The pass will grant holders access to three exclusive NFT artwork drops by world-class artists in 2024, exclusive access to online and offline experiences, access to surprise and delight bonus drops, and entry into raffles for official Oracle Red Bull Racing prizes.

We were able to speak to Kjetil Golid, one of the Season 2 artists, exclusively for this book. He told us:

> *Last year's Velocity series featured some highly talented and respected artists, so it was an honour for me to be offered a spot in this year's lineup. I've also been a long-time fan and follower of Formula 1, so when I got presented with the opportunity to make a project with a top team like ORBR, I immediately accepted, and began thinking of ways to incorporate the aspects that fascinate me with the sport into a piece of art.*

Oracle Red Bull Racing saw the success of what is now Season 1 as an important factor in bringing back the Velocity Pass for a second season in 2024, also underscoring the value and appreciation both for the artistry and exclusivity offered through this collaboration between Bybit Web3, AOI and ORBR. Furthermore, it highlights the interesting crossover potential and bridging the gap between Formula 1 and the burgeoning NFT space, nurturing a new generation of enthusiasts and collectors. It will continue to push the boundaries of digital art by introducing 'Data-Driven Art'. The new series embraces the fusion of art and racing, featuring unique digital art collections inspired by real-time data and the exhilarating achievements of the iconic RB20 F1 car. Meanwhile, in a bold industry move, Bybit Web3 and Oracle Red Bull Racing will launch fractional NFTs on the DN-404 (Divisible NFT-404) protocol for the first time in 2024. This means that holders will also be able to fractionalise and trade their passes using this new smart contract protocol (DN-404), which allows fans to participate on a much bigger scale. ORBR is the first big brand using this tech and pushing the boundaries of what is possible in the space.

Why is this both interesting and innovative? NFTs are usually ERC-721 tokens. This is the 'non-fungible token standard'. ERC-20 tokens, though, are fungible. DN-404 is a new standard known as the 'divisible NFT', which allows for the fractionalisation of NFTs. It aims at combining the functionalities of ERC-20 and 721 token standards by creating a 'semi-fungible token', which will allow for more liquid NFT markets, more seamless fractionalisation of assets and more akin to a coin that can be more easily sold. It is also an interesting new way of creating further access points into Velocity while maintaining the scarcity.

The quotes below are from key contributors to the project in Oracle Red Bull Racing, Art on Internet and DN-404.

As a team, we're continuing to use Web3 technology and innovation to reach new fans, build hyper-engaged communities, create brand advocates, and tap into a new world of sport fandom. New world brand values and emerging tech are the ultimate creative canvas to build with our fans, not just for them, while rewarding them along the way. This is why I am so passionate about Oracle Red Bull Racing's Velocity Series.

Dan Mitchell, Senior Marketing Manager
(Fan Engagement), exclusively for this chapter

Building on the success of the first Velocity Pass, we're excited to push the boundaries of artistic expression even further. This series bridges the gap between artistic expression and the data-driven world of F1, offering fresh perspectives on the sport we love.

Federica from AOI in a launch announcement,
April 2024

DN-404 is proud to be the technological backbone of the Velocity Pass Series 2.0. Our secure and cost-efficient new protocol ensures a seamless experience for fans collecting these incredible pieces of digital art.

Pop Punk from DN-404 in a launch announcement, April 2024

In summary, I chose Oracle Red Bull Racing as one of the three brand case studies as there is clearly some continuity, consistency and commitment to the Velocity Pass programme. This is a testament to the success of its first season that it wanted to repeat it again for Season 2, which is set to be even bigger and better. It is also an established brand that has a more famous footprint on the race track in Formula 1 and is seeking to bring that sense of tribalism, hardcore fandom and community over to the web3 space. Its efforts are also to be applauded in appealing to a few different audiences, from artist collectors and curious traders to fans of the bleeding edge with DN-404.[34]

CASE STUDY 2 – ADIDAS INTO THE METAVERSE

In December 2021, adidas launched a high-profile NFT collection which sold out in seconds and generated £18.11 million ($23 million) in one day for the company.[35] Adidas collaborated with well-known pioneers in the NFT space, such as Bored Apes and PUNK Comics, and partnered with gmoney for strategic guidance. At the time, it was heralded as the yardstick for brands to seek to emulate both in their entrance to the space, the scale of the offering and its future vision of

---

34 Bybit (2024) *Bybit and Oracle Red Bull racing ignite excitement with Velocity Series 2.0: Unveiling innovative divisible, data-driven ART NFTS, PR Newswire: news distribution, targeting and monitoring.* Available at: www.prnewswire.com/in/news-releases/bybit-and-oracle-red-bull-racing-ignite-excitement-with-velocity-series-2-0-unveiling-innovative-divisible-data-driven-art-nfts-302112681.html.

35 *Into the metaverse: How we got here and where we are headed* (2021) *adidas News Site.* Available at: https://news.adidas.com/originals/into-the-metaverse--how-we-got-here-and-where-we-are-headed/s/6ccb61cb-2135-453e-8626-ac3d56faab30.

where it could go.[36] All brands eager to do the same looked to adidas for learnings and best practices.

Adidas entered the metaverse/web3/NFT space in such a way that immediately made people watch and learn, with the right body language and early voyager intent, with the right cultural nous to show that they were doing this from a good place and with authenticity. On its launch Erika Wykes-Sneyd said, 'Today we are marking our intent for web3 with into the metaverse, an exclusive NFT drop of digital and physical products.'[37]

It was also one of the first major brands to create a dedicated Discord server to keep their community up to date and have a closer direct consumer relationship. On 20 January 2022, the brand launched its official Discord channel, which rapidly grew and within six months, had reached 59,000 members.

Adidas also launched a limited merchandise collection, exclusively for holders of their NFT token, further amplifying the sense of exclusivity and giving fans the opportunity to own both digital and physical brand artefacts.

Adidas started with 30,000 NFTs available for sale, which all sold out in seconds. At the time, Tareq Naslawy said of the initiative, 'We want to figure out what would be the dopest thing to do in the space and start involving the communities we're activating through the NFT in how we should manifest in the digital world.'[38]

36 Person (2023) How adidas launched its NFT collection generating $23M in just one day, RightMetric. Available at: https://rightmetric.co/insight-library/how-adidas-launched-its-nft-collection-generating-23m-in-just-one-day

37 Into the metaverse: How we got here and where we are headed (2021a) adidas News Site | Press Resources for all Brands, Sports and Innovations. Available at: https://news.adidas.com/originals/into-the-metaverse--how-we-got-here-and-where-we-are-headed/s/6ccb61cb-2135-453e-8626-ac3d56faab30.

38 Kastrenakes, J. (2021) *adidas is launching an NFT collection with exclusive access to Streetwear drops, The Verge.* Available at: www.theverge.com/2021/12/16/22822143/adidas-nft-launch-into-the-metaverse-price-release-date.

The NFT holder exclusive hoodie adidas created, shows the 0x contract address alongside icons for influencer gmoney, Bored Ape Yacht Club, Punks Comics and adidas. Most notably, for the first time in their history, adidas flipped their trefoil logo on its side for the web3 initiative. In addition to the hoodie, holders also got an 'iconic adicolor Firebird tracksuit', and gmoney's classic orange beanie.

The NFTs sold for 0.2 ETH each, which at the time, was around $800. 'The intent is this thing, this NFT, you belong to a community, and we continue to add value to that over time, and it is gonna also evolve with what we're learning about the community, how they're changing and evolving,' Erika Wykes-Sneyd told The Verge in December 2021.[39]

We were able to receive two exclusives from adidas just for this book, the first being an exclusive quote from Erika Wykes-Sneyd, Global Vice President and GM of adidas /// studio, and the second being a full timeline of all web3 brand activations since launch in November 2021 through to April 2024 from the adidas Three Stripes Studio. As time has passed, it is easy to forget just how many activations have been part of this multi-year commitment to web3 by adidas. Erika Wykes-Sneyd, Global Vice President and GM of adidas /// studio told us exclusively:

We were the first global sport-lifestyle brand to launch an NFT during the bull market run of 2021. Since then we have created a global community establishing the largest brand-led Discord, conducted dozens of onchain pilots and established a business unit to monetise virtual goods across onchain gaming, phygital products and collectables. We have always approached the space with a long-term view but act in a manner that generates near-term revenue and credibility for adidas. Where other brands see the impossible, we use that as our opportunity to establish meaningful relationships with the builders and creators of the new internet culture. This is the cradle of the emerging creator economy. Now is the time to get in and build.

39 Ibid.

The key moments for adidas' web3 foray span from November 2021 all the way through to April 2024. Where you see ITM, it refers to Into the Metaverse, the launch campaign.

- November 2021
  - Adidas Originals Web3 Manifesto and POAP easter egg in CONFIRMED app
  - Strategic partnerships announced with The Sandbox (virtual land acquisition) and Coinbase (digital wallet set up)
  - Adidas Originals purchases BAYC NFT #8774 (creation of Indigo Herz character)
- December 2021
  - Indigo Herz integrated into Punks Comics edition #2. 10,000 NFTs sold in under 20 minutes
  - 'Into the Metaverse' (ITM) NFT launch: Partnership with BAYC, Punks Comic and gmoney – selling 30,000 NFTs
- January 2022
  - Adidas for Prada re-source creator-owned NFT in collaboration with Zach Lieberman
  - Adidas Discord Servers
- March 2022
  - Adidas part of Yuga Labs funding round, Indigo Herz featured next to other brands
  - Sandbox Alpha Pass Giveaway for Alpha Season 2 – 200 passes to ITM holders
  - Indigo Herz featured in Sandbox Alpha Season 2
- April 2022
  - First NFT raffle on the CONFIRMED app – 50 ITM NFTs
  - ITM Phase 1: Forging event claim physical merch (hoodie, tracksuit, beanie)

- May 2022
  - ITM Phase 2: Kick off – request to burn Phase 1 NFT for Phase 2
- June 2022
  - ITM Phase 2: Airdrop of adidas Originals Meta Capsule NFT to all Phase 2 holders (24,000 NFTs)
  - Launch of dedicated adidas web3 Twitter account – Indigo Herz account
- July 2022
  - Wagmi Utd NFT drop with adidas merch
- October 2022
  - ITM Phase 2: Transition of adidas Originals Meta Capsule NFT to Impossible Box NFT
- November 2022
  - ITM Phase 2: Unveil of adidas Virtual Gear (digital only wearables)
- December 2022
  - ITM Phase 2: Art Basel Miami Community Party to celebrate adidas Virtual Gear
- January 2023
  - /// studio – Dedicated team created to manage all web3 activations
- February 2023
  - Community Council (15 individuals chosen to be community champions)
- March 2023
  - Metaverse Fashion Week Decentraland – Voted #1 experience (to highlight adidas Virtual Gear)
  - ITM Phase 3 Rebrand to ALTs by adidas (PFP)
  - ALTS by adidas – Community event Berlin and community artist and art launched (RAWS)

- April 2023
  - ALTS by adidas – Chapter 1: Universal key sale and introduction of ALT(er) Egos (collect first PFP trait)
  - ALTS by adidas – Community event NYC (NFT NYC) and community artist and art launched (Mike Fogg)
  - Tokenproof integration into CONFIRMED app for digital wallet creation
  - Indigo Herz Merch Pack (footwear and apparel) incl. token gated access for ALTS
  - Golden Ticket NFT during adiClub Members Week
- May-July 2023
  - ALTs by adidas: Chapter 2 – Rift Valley Motel Coins and Vending Machine (collect second PFP trait – facial traits)
- August 2023
  - Adidas Originals x BAPE – Limited Edition Sneaker Auction (Forum Triple-Whites – only 100 units globally)
- September 2023
  - Launch of 'Residency' – Artist in residency programme to support upcoming and emerging artists
  - Launch of 'Residency' x Seoul Korea Blockchain Week – selling art of upcoming artists Monkeemoto and DearNostalgia
  - ALTS by adidas: Chapter 3: Trait swapping and upgrades (related to second PFP trait)
- October 2023
  - NFT integration into main adidas Originals x Moncler campaign – airdrop of a Digital Moncler NFT Boot via the CONFIRMED App
- November 2023
  - Adidas Football x Bugatti – Limited Edition Football Boot NFT Auction (only 99 units globally)

- December 2023
    - ALTS by adidas: Year End Giveaway – 12 days of giveaways
- April 2024
    - STEPN x adidas Solana NFTs: Genesis Collection of 1,000 running inspired.

In summary, I chose adidas and its Into the Metaverse web3 initiative as one of the three brand case studies due to it being one of **the** brand moments within web3 at the time that made people and other brands start to take notice of this emerging ecosystem. Adidas can always be remembered for being the pioneer and for breaking new ground before any other major brand. For that, it will always have the provenance and the feeling of 'we were there'. Seeing the timeline above of activations since it launched in November 2021 also reinforces its internal buy-in and commitment at the highest level with a multi-year programme of events.

It was also one of the first major brands to signal its intent to be part of the culture by purchasing ape #8774 from the Bored Ape Yacht Club at a time of peak popularity where this brand body language saw it find whole new audiences and demographics to reach. Congratulations adidas for your inclusion.

CASE STUDY 3 – AUSTRALIAN TENNIS OPEN ARTBALL 2022

In January 2022, the Australian Open became the first grand slam to create a series of NFTs (AO ArtBall NFTs) that were linked to real-world live match data, giving people around the world a unique opportunity to own a piece of the Australian Open. It was billed as 'the ball that has it all'.

At the same time, it also created a virtual experience within the 3D virtual reality platform Decentraland with the ambition of creating a greater sense of accessibility and experience to those not able to be there in person, allowing any tennis fan wherever they are in the world to explore the AO. Chief Commercial Officer Cedric Cornelis said in an official announcement:

The Australian Open prides itself on being one of the most innovative sports and entertainment events in the world, and we are delighted that through our expansion into the Metaverse and Decentraland, more fans can engage with our sport than ever before. We work closely with some of the world's best developers to ensure we stay ahead of consumer trends and continue to expand into new sectors in ways never before seen in tennis.[40]

Meanwhile, Ridley Plummer, Tennis Australia Senior Manager for Digital Sales and Metaverse continued:

We want the AO to be the world's most accessible and inclusive sports and entertainment event, and with the unique challenges fans have faced getting to Melbourne, we've fast-tracked our launch into the Metaverse. Taking the AO into the Metaverse is an important step to provide truly global access to our great event – we couldn't have done that without the amazing collaborators we've had on the project, in particular the team from Vegas City, who have worked tirelessly on the build.[41]

The NFT project consisted of 6,776 AO ArtBall NFTs that were created (minted) in 2022 which at the time was a pioneering moment due to the reach they get, with almost 1 billion global views to AO properties, making it a unique opportunity to own a part of the moment. In 2023, it introduced additional benefits that were communicated through a 'litepaper' and sold a further 2,454 new NFTs.

---

40 Ausopen.com, 1 (2022) *Ao launches into Metaverse, serves up world-first NFT art collection linked to live match data, AO.* Available at: https://ausopen.com/articles/news/ao-launches-metaverse-serves-world-first-nft-art-collection-linked-live-match-data.

41 Ibid.

The most interesting aspect to me was the fact that the metadata of these initial 6,776 NFTs were each linked to a 19cm x 19cm plot of the tennis court surface at the Australian Open. If the winning shot from any of the 400+ AO matches lands on that 19cm x 19cm plot, the NFT metadata will be updated accordingly, in real time to highlight the match information.

Additionally, the NFTs offered extra perks like limited-edition wearables, AO merchandise and other promised future benefits.

It was all made possible by official match and ball-tracking data from AO matches. Until this time, combining real-time court data with NFTs had never been attempted.

It introduced new opportunities for global tennis fans to engage as NFT holders with AO. For example, if one of the 11 championship points lands on a plot, the NFT owner of that plot can claim the tennis ball used in the championship point, presented in a specially handcrafted case.

ArtBall holders who lived in Australia also had the ability to redeem free tickets for the in-person games. 'The court plot tied to the NFT will be revealed when the balls are minted, meaning a buyer can't choose a specific position on-court. Down the line shots and the ace down the T are where you'll want to be,' said Run It Wild Founder, Adam De Cata.[42]

Along with it being a first-of-its-kind project in many ways (NFTs linked to real-time match data), the ArtBalls themselves were generatively produced.

The algorithmic blend of various colour schemes, patterns and textures ensured that each AO ArtBall was unique in appearance, even down to the fuzz on the ball.

---

[42] Ibid.

Within the collection are 22 AO 'Legend' designs, which were handcrafted from historical AO artwork. This includes the 'Serving Man' silhouette, first introduced in the 1997 Australian Open, which has been revived and reinterpreted on an ArtBall canvas. These have a much greater rarity due to the limitations of distribution put in place, with only 22 of the series having these traits.

The AO ArtBalls also feature over 160 NFTs from the AO Artist Series, showcasing designs specifically created for AO 2022 by both local and international artists.

The project was such a success that it picked up a Bronze Lion for most innovative use of tech and platforms in sport at Cannes Lions, winning the first Cannes Lions for an NFT–metaverse project in the entertainment category for sports. It has continued as a yearly activation ever since with iterations so far in 2023 and to come in 2024. In official 2024 marketing, it is billed as 'the ball that has it all'.

On winning the award, Ridley Plummer said:

> It is a huge honour as a web3 project to be recognised by the creative industry in the most prestigious creative awards. We wanted to push the boundaries of what was possible using the technology we had available to us – we believe our ability to link data, sport and technology to drive a valuable consumer experience is true innovation.[43]

One such illustration, showcasing the additional utility, value, exclusivity and desire of owning one of the NFTs, became apparent when, in June 2022, NFT holders were invited to an AO Metaverse crypto-can't-buy private tennis clinic with Stan Smith of adidas fame, a former world number one tennis player, two-time major singles champion and from one of the most successful doubles pairings of all time.

---

43 Regan, A. (2022) *A 'crazy ride' to a Cannes Lions for Australian open Metaverse NFT, AdNews.* Available at: www.adnews.com.au/news/a-crazy-ride-to-a-cannes-lions-for-australian-open-metaverse-nft.

In a further show of strength for the AO ArtBall rewards programme, every holder was able to claim a pair of complimentary Seven Day Ground Passes for week two of AO23. Given there were 6,776 AO ArtBalls in circulation at the time, it represented the largest release of tickets to an AO membership programme in the history of the event. Holders of more than one AO ArtBall were able to claim multiple pairs of ground passes based on the number of balls they own, capped at 20 tickets. Other benefits include access to other major international sporting events, web3 conferences, behind-the-scenes streams at the AO, limited edition merchandise and more.

In 2023, it expanded the virtual gaming experience further still, outside of NFTs and into Roblox, with a whole host of brand partners. This included an Emirates-sponsored obstacle course, ESPN-branded tennis game and more recently, Dunlop Tennis Ball Rain and a Ralph Lauren ball kids kit and retail store. In April 2024, it was reported that the AO adventure gaming experience on Roblox was the number one sporting experience with over 670,000 visitors in April 2024 alone and total lifetime visits of 17.7 million from over 7.5 million unique users worldwide. In a series of posts on LinkedIn, Ridley Plummer said:

AO Adventure continues to grow and lead Tennis Australia's strategy to make the AO the world's most accessible sports and entertainment event. We believe 'playing' makes life better, while our vision is to create a playful world through tennis for everyone. The objectives of AO Adventure are simple. Engage with a global audience that knows tennis, but may not be familiar with the AO – building brand awareness and ongoing brand affinity. Extend the AO beyond 2 weeks in January using a 24/7, always-on model to give the AO brand and our partners ongoing exposure. And continue to build the World's largest sports and entertainment event. Collaboration is also a key to our success here. A big thank you to our new collaborators for AO24, ESPN and Wimbledon, along with our ongoing partners Emirates, US Open and Dunlop Sports.

And of course, our development partners at The Gang and Doppelgänger.[44]

In summary, the Australian Open ArtBall was a groundbreaking innovation that utilised real match data from the tournament. The court was divided into 6,776 squares, each linked to a tennis ball NFT which had never been done before. These NFTs would update based on where points were scored during the tournament, making it an industry first.

As a company, it has continued to be an innovator in new and emerging platforms in the years and activations since AO ArtBall's inception in 2022, reaching new heights (and audiences) via Roblox and others since. AO ArtBall was a world-first in combining NFT art with real-time court data to create a dynamic NFT. The project offered global tennis AO fans to engage with experiences like never before, from anywhere in the world. It was an industry and category-defining activation that also caught the attention of Cannes Lions, where it received the winner for 'Innovative Use of Tech & Platforms for Sport' in 2022. The Cannes Lions Awards, held annually, is the world's most esteemed benchmark for creative excellence. Creative companies from over 90 countries submit more than 30,000 works across 28 categories each year.

A few other success metrics: its public sale sold out in 3 minutes and 2 seconds, receiving 1,000+ ETH of secondary trading volume within 48 hours and was one of the top 100 projects at the time on OpenSea.

On winning the Cannes Lion award, Adam De Cata, CEO of NFT Tech and Founder of Run It Wild had this to say:

I'm incredibly proud of what the Run It Wild team has delivered – being recognized for a project that was anchored by

---

44 Plummer, R. (2024) *Ridley Plummer on LinkedIn:* Available at: www.linkedin.com/feed/update/urn:li:activity:7196773174577950721/.

blockchain technology, there's something truly beautiful when creative, data and technology meet. Having the faith and support of the AO, it is been a crazy ride pushing the limits of creative and technological possibilities, elevating those we work with. [...] Accepting this award in the same category as major brands like adidas, Nike, and Samsung reinforces the power of web3 and its possibilities.[45]

45 NFT Tech (2023) *NFT Tech's Run it wild and AO Metaverse win Cannes Lions Award for Sports Entertainment, RSS.* Available at: www.nfttech.com/newsroom/nft-techs-run-it-wild-and-ao-metaverse-win-cannes-lions-award-for-sports-entertainment.

8 Safety, security and wallets relating to NFTs

This chapter delves into the critical aspects of safety, security and wallets in the NFT ecosystem, providing a comprehensive guide for both the novice user and a cautionary reminder for experienced users.

The explosive growth of NFTs has revolutionised the digital financial world, offering a new approach for owning and trading digital assets. The advent of Decentralised Finance, commonly referred to as DeFi, represents a paradigm shift in the financial industry. It utilises blockchain technology to establish a financial system that is open, transparent and accessible to everyone with an internet connection. Unlike traditional financial systems, which rely on intermediaries such as banks and brokers, DeFi operates on decentralised platforms, removing the need for these middlemen.

However, with these great innovations comes the need for even more stringent safety, security and risk management measures, and sadly these are not adhered to by all, which is why scams, hacks, wallet drains and bad actors are all rife. There has also never been a time in history when such power, responsibility and funds were under the sole stewardship of the individual without any/many safeguards. This is one of the big risks and drawbacks in the utopian dream of true decentralisation where there is no entity that safeguards your funds and you, as an individual, have full control. With that comes a heightened level of risk, which some may not be aware of or mindful of in their quest for achieving financial freedom.

A cryptocurrency wallet can be thought of as a digital password holder that enables access to one's digital assets, which are stored on the blockchain. These keys ('passwords') are alphanumeric strings, one private (which should never be shared, for sending cryptocurrency) and one public (which can be shared, for receiving cryptocurrency). Wallets also come with a secret or 'seed' phrase, which commonly takes the form of a list of words that is used to derive the private key. Crypto wallets also do not contain cryptocurrency themselves, however, their keys are used to identify and execute transactions on the blockchain.

Wallets are effectively composed of three key parts:

A public address – by default, a string of alphanumeric characters derived from the public key. It is used to receive cryptocurrency transactions. Some users may choose to purchase an 'ENS' address, which effectively creates a 'vanity' address. This is much easier to use, interact with and share. For example, mine is mlitman.eth instead of 0x241a95bfF01c3C807b9EeD7d3bEe8dFDf27FEfF1.

A private key – a randomly generated string of alphanumeric characters that allows the holder to access and manage the cryptocurrency stored in the wallet. Private keys play a pivotal role in ensuring the security and integrity of crypto transactions. It is typically a 256-bit number and will look something like this: 5Kb8kLf9zgWQnogidDA76MzPL6TsZZY36hWXMssSzNyd YXYB9KF.

A seed phrase – to recover the private key. Also known as a recovery phrase or mnemonic phrase, it is a series of 12, 18 or 24 words generated when a wallet is created. It can be used to restore access to the wallet. Important note: you must never share your wallet seed phrase with anyone. Think of this as the key to your house and you cannot get in without it. The seed phrase can regenerate the private key and by extension, access to the cryptocurrency. This makes it essential for wallet recovery.

A crypto wallet's functionality hinges on the interplay between the public address, private key and seed phrase, as mentioned above. Understanding and securely managing these components is crucial for anyone involved in cryptocurrency transactions. By keeping the private key and seed phrase secure, users can protect their assets and ensure they can always regain access to their wallet if necessary.

Within web3, a user can sign into and use various apps such as Uniswap (a trading platform) with their wallets (for example, MetaMask, Rainbow and others) or sign in to marketplaces like OpenSea, Magic Eden and others only needing their (crypto) wallet to do so. Think of it like logging in to a site using your email address.

As a business, NFTs need to be deployed by a wallet. It is generally a security risk to have a single wallet control an NFT. For this reason, multisignature wallets exist, where multiple people have to sign a transaction for it to go through. As a result of this, most NFT projects use a multisig wallet.

TYPES OF WALLETS

There are also many different types of wallets, whether they are custodial or non-custodial wallets; the next consideration is whether the wallet is hot (for example, MetaMask) or cold (for example, a Ledger physical hardware wallet). The key difference between custodial and non-custodial (or self-custodial) wallets lies in who possesses the keys contained in the wallet. With a custodial wallet, a third party manages the cryptocurrency owner's transactions and private keys. Non-custodial means the user maintains ownership of the keys.

Custodial – Similar to trusting money to a bank, the keys are held by wallet providers. Coinbase is an example of a custodial wallet.

Pros

- No need to worry about managing keys.

- Customer support is available for questions and technical support.

- Access to benefits such as earning interest or rewards simply for holding the funds there.

Cons

- Custodians can lose funds through hacks or exploits, such as the Mt.Gox hack.

- Risk of custodians going bankrupt, in which case funds may be at risk (see: FTX).

Non-custodial – This is similar to storing money in a safe that only you have access to. MetaMask is an example of a non-custodial wallet.

Pros

- Full control and ownership over assets maintained, totally decentralised.

- Used in most web3 applications.

Cons

- Higher risk of phishing and hacks due to not having a company to contact if any problems accessing funds.

- A greater ability to lose assets by forgetting or losing keys.

HOT OR COLD (WALLET)?

The biggest difference between a hot and a cold wallet is its connectivity and accessibility. A hot wallet is always connected to the internet, making it more convenient for frequent transactions and it can also connect freely with dApps. A dApp is essentially a blockchain-integrated website that requires you to connect and approve all transactions with your wallet signature. dApps have been developed to decentralise a range of functions and applications and eliminate intermediaries. They have transformed how we engage, exchange and entertain. Examples include Uniswap (a currency exchange service that allows users to trade coins directly with each other), Compound (a lending protocol allowing users to borrow and lend using crypto coins) and OpenSea (a marketplace for buying, selling and trading NFTs).

Using a hot wallet is the most optimal solution though, suitable for daily transactions, active trading and convenience but exercising a high level of personal responsibility in trusting the sites and apps that you are connecting to. However, due to a hot wallet's constant connection to the internet, the former is more susceptible to hacking, phishing attacks, draining and other security breaches.

A cold wallet is a type of cryptocurrency wallet designed to securely store digital assets offline. Unlike hot wallets, which are connected to the internet and susceptible to hacking, cold wallets offer a higher level of security by keeping the private keys that control cryptocurrency access completely offline. Ledger, a leading brand in this space, produces hardware wallets that resemble USB drives. These devices allow users to store their private keys in a secure, offline environment while still enabling transactions when connected to a computer or mobile device. To execute a transaction, the user must physically connect the Ledger wallet and authorise the transfer, adding an extra layer of protection against unauthorised access. This makes cold wallets like Ledger an ideal choice for long-term storage of cryptocurrencies and safeguarding significant amounts of digital assets.

The downside of this is that accessing funds from a cold wallet is less convenient and can be slower as it requires physical access to the storage device. Cold storage is the most optimal solution for long-term storage, though, and for holding large amounts of cryptocurrency that do not need to be accessed frequently.

Examples of cold wallets available include those from Ledger (Nano S Plus, X, Flex or Stax) Trezor (Model T, Safe 3) and NGRAVE (Zero).

It is often recommended to use both hot and cold wallets. A hot wallet, for example, MetaMask, is likely to be used more frequently day to day than a cold wallet, for example, Ledger, but you can then also send NFTs or crypto from your hot wallet across to your cold storage for safekeeping.

As you can see, custodial or non-custodial and hot or cold each have their own key use cases and pros and cons. As previously mentioned, it is effectively up to the user how much control and risk they want to expose themselves to. Ultimately, this means that it is both a good and a bad thing that with decentralisation it is up to the user to self-police and protect themselves both with a hot and cold wallet, as they are the ones who hold the keys to their wallet.

Hardware wallet provider Ledger, which produces 'cold' storage hardware devices, uses the line 'Not your keys, not your crypto' in its marketing to encourage people to take full (self) custody of their crypto, hold the keys themselves and keep their assets safe. Self-custody is the bedrock of crypto, embodying the principle of decentralisation. It means you hold the keys to your digital assets, rather than a third party doing so. Imagine having a digital safe deposit box accessible only by you. Ledger devices include the Nano S Plus/X or the recently released Stax which started shipping out to pre-orders across three batches on 28 May 2024 after a long-publicised wait. They expect to be available for general sale by September 2024.

Why is this such big news? The Ledger Stax was originally announced in December 2022 to much fanfare by Tony Fadell, creator of the iPod. They expected to ship in Q1 2023 but encountered numerous issues and challenges with the manufacturing and production of this world's first-of-its-kind secure, touchscreen device. It is expected to bring significant upgrades to how it is used and interacted with, including the device's intuitiveness and an overall 'cool' factor.

It does look to be shaping up to be worth the wait, featuring many industry firsts. It includes the first secure touchscreen and the first time a touchscreen user interface has been driven by a secure element chip, which is crucial for crypto security. It is also the first curved E-Ink display ever built, the first display using organic semiconductor materials on plastic substrates rather than silicon materials on glass, and the only screen made at less than 100 degrees. 'Most devices in the past have lacked security, or they've lacked utility – or they haven't had enough visual space for you to see what it is you're signing,' says Ledger CXO, Ian Rogers (@iancr) on X,[46] on officially announcing Stax starting to ship out for pre-ordered customers, of which some have been waiting over a year. It is a major step towards making digital ownership easily accessible to anyone and not just the tech-savvy. While the web3 space still remains in its infancy, it is one of the unfortunate byproducts of both the quest for decentralisation and the opportunity for some to achieve extreme wealth opportunities in nefarious ways, as such scams are common and far-reaching. Ledger Stax seeks to make these much less of a common occurrence. Pascal Gauthier, CEO, Ledger, said:

Within the next few years, the crypto revolution will reshape how hundreds of millions of people own and manage all value, but as I've said on multiple occasions, our smart-phones and laptops lack fundamental security features to let us onboard this era. People need intuitive devices combining security, ownership, and privacy to manage their digital value with control, free from compromise.[47]

---

46 *X.com* (2024) *X (formerly Twitter)*. Available at: https://x.com/Ledger/status/1795334290378576382.

47 Gauthier, P. (2024) Ledger Stax now shipping: A message from Ledger's CEO Pascal Gauthier, Ledger. Available at: www.ledger.com/blog-ledger-stax-now-shipping-a-message-from-ledgers-ceo-pascal-gauthier.

There are ultimately three key fail points regarding safety when using crypto and the blockchain.

1. **Personal safety:** Protecting personal information from phishing attacks and social engineering.

2. **Asset safety:** Ensuring the security of digital assets from hacks and unauthorised access.

3. **Transaction safety:** Verifying the authenticity and legitimacy of NFT transactions to avoid scams and fraud.

The most common threats when seeking to safeguard your NFTs are as follows:

1. **Phishing attacks:** Malicious actors often use phishing techniques to trick users into revealing their private keys or seed phrases.

2. **Smart contract vulnerabilities:** Bugs or vulnerabilities in smart contracts can be exploited, leading to loss of assets.

3. **Marketplace scams:** Fraudulent listings and counterfeit NFTs are prevalent in online marketplaces.

In web3, it is unfortunate that if funds are accidentally sent or NFTs are sent to a malicious party, there is no way to get them back. It can be very unforgiving and extensive funds can be lost when mistakenly connecting to what looks like a legitimate site but is actually a clone designed only to drain users' wallet funds.

Teams that are creating projects do share some responsibility, too. For example, if a project does not properly secure its Discord server, a hacker could come in and post a phishing site through official channels requesting users to connect their wallets to a fake site, only for the wallet to be wholly drained. This is generally seen as the project's responsibility.

Securing your NFTs requires a multi-faceted approach involving best practices, tools and awareness:

1. **Use reputable wallets:** Choose wallets that are well-reviewed and widely used within the community, such as those mentioned above, for example, MetaMask, Coinbase Wallet, Rainbow or Phantom (hot) and Ledger, Trezor or NGRAVE (cold) see referenced earlier in the chapter.

2. **Enable Two-Factor Authentication (2FA):** Add an extra layer of security by enabling 2FA on your accounts.

3. **Regular updates:** Keep your wallet software and any associated applications up to date to protect against known vulnerabilities.

4. **Secure backups:** Store backups of your seed phrases in multiple, secure, offline locations.

5. **Finally, the most important one:** If it looks or sounds too good to be true, it usually is.

Setting up an NFT wallet involves several steps to ensure maximum security:

1. **Download from official sources:** Always download wallet software from official websites or trusted app stores.

2. **Create a new wallet:** Follow the setup process to create a new wallet, generating a unique seed phrase.

3. **Secure the seed phrase:** Write down the seed phrase and store it in a secure, offline location. Never share your seed phrase with anyone.

4. **Fund your wallet:** Add funds (cryptocurrency) to your wallet to start buying and trading NFTs.

Conducting NFT transactions safely requires vigilance and adherence to best practices:

1. **Verify contract addresses:** Always verify the smart contract address of the NFT you are purchasing.

2. **Double-check transaction details:** Ensure the details of your transaction are correct before confirming.

The NFT landscape is continually evolving, with new threats and vulnerabilities emerging regularly. Staying informed and vigilant is crucial:

1. **Follow trusted sources:** Keep up with news and updates from trusted sources within the NFT community.

2. **Participate in community discussions:** Engage with other users and experts in forums and social media groups to share knowledge and experiences.

3. **Educate yourself continuously:** Update your knowledge regularly about new security practices and tools.

In summary, while that all might sound and feel daunting, overwhelming and perplexing, it is important to know the differences and considerations when it comes to different types of wallets to ensure you are as safe and secure as you can be. While there are clear benefits of decentralised finance, it does mean that there is more responsibility and risk with the end user, which some may not be aware of. Navigating the NFT ecosystem safely and securely requires a proactive approach to understanding and mitigating risks. By using reputable wallets, adhering to best practices and staying informed, you can protect your digital assets and enjoy the benefits of this revolutionary technology. Remember, in the world of NFTs, security is paramount and taking the necessary steps to safeguard your investments is essential for a successful and enjoyable experience.

9 Blockchains and their different uses

The blockchain landscape, when it comes to NFTs, is rapidly evolving in 2024 and is seeing far greater choice and optionality for consumers now than in previous years. We will touch on Ethereum, Solana, Bitcoin, Avalanche and Polygon as the top five. Hold on to your hats though. This one is going to be probably the most technical of the chapters as we look at the key benefits of each of the top blockchains.

ETHEREUM

Across 2021–2022, within NFTs, Ethereum was the king of them all, with gas prices (the cost to transact) often being hundreds of dollars at the busiest of times on top of whatever you were buying. The most famous example of this inefficiency showing its ugly side was in May 2022 for Otherdeeds by Yuga Labs, which are NFTs for digital land related to an upcoming metaverse gaming project called Otherside. The primary issue with the Otherside mint was the high gas fees, which cover the computational expenses of validating transactions under Ethereum's proof-of-work protocol. In this version of Ethereum, the 'base fee' of a transaction is burned, essentially sent to an unusable address, while any additional tip is given to the miner as an incentive for quicker transaction confirmation. These fees can surge dramatically during high-demand events, as users seek expedited

transaction processing and the miners also want to be the quickest to the transaction to win the fees. This leads to 'gas wars', where escalating bids for transaction speed drive up fees for all Ethereum users, causing network congestion and bottlenecks due to increased load.

What ended up happening in May 2022 still leaves a sour taste over two years later for those who participated, when the sheer numbers of people trying to get their own piece of digital land effectively 'clogged' the Ethereum blockchain. This effectively caused the aforementioned 'gas war' with people trying to pay increasingly more gas (purchase tax) to front-run others and be first to the purchase, so much so, that many transactions failed and cost a combined wastage of approximately $180 million. Incidentally, two years later, in May 2024, the Otherside game has not yet launched. Yuga Labs first pivoted hard into gaming, hiring former Activision CEO and gaming heavy hitter Daniel Alegre, who joined the company in April 2023 to spearhead its metaverse gaming vision. At the time, this was seen to be a pivotal hire that brought credibility, authority and trust, before winding back on this hire less than a year later with Greg Solana stepping back into the CEO role in February 2024 and issuing a rallying cry both internally and externally that it is going back to its crypto native roots and removing corporate layers of bureaucracy that had crept into the company.

Now there are many more options and therefore liquidity is spread in many more directions. This also plays a part in Ethereum-only NFTs prices dropping as funds are pulled out and held elsewhere.

That said, Ethereum continues to lead with the largest ecosystem of dApps and consistent development activities, especially with its transition to Ethereum 2.0 which brought better scalability and energy efficiency. As a result, we will likely never again see a (gas) moment like the Otherdeeds mint of 2022.

SOLANA

In 2024, Solana experienced one of its key breakout moments for a few reasons:

1. after being decoupled from FTX as the disastrous chain of events that saw Sam Bankman-Fried jailed for 25 years for defrauding billions of customer funds;

2. in part, thanks to the memecoin craze, including the likes of $WIF, $EPIK, $PEPE and political-themed memecoins including $TREMP and $BODEN taking significant volumes of users' time and dollars;

3. gaming;

4. decentralised finance (DeFi).

On a practical level, Solana has also successfully taken market share away from Ethereum due to its extremely fast time to process and transfer transactions and also its almost zero transaction fees per purchase which would more likely be nothing more than a fraction of a dollar. This is a big culture shock compared with gas fees on Ethereum at their heyday anywhere from $1–200, but more likely anything from $1–20 now at busier times.

Solana has gained significant attention due to its unique features and capabilities:

1. **High throughput and speed**: Solana is capable of processing tens of thousands of transactions per second (TPS) thanks to its innovative consensus mechanism, Proof of History (PoH). This mechanism allows for greater scalability and faster transaction times compared to many other blockchains.

2. **Low transaction costs:** Despite its high throughput, Solana maintains very low transaction costs, which makes it an attractive platform for developers and businesses looking to build and operate dApps without incurring high fees.

3. **Consensus mechanism:** Solana uses a unique combination of Proof of Stake (PoS) and PoH, a timekeeping technique that helps to secure the network and order transactions more efficiently, reducing the need for communication between nodes to verify transaction orders.

4. **Developer-friendly:** Solana supports a variety of programming languages, including Rust and C, which are popular among systems programmers for their control over system resources and performance. This makes it easier for developers to build and deploy high-performance applications.

5. **Use cases:** Solana is widely used for various applications, particularly in areas where speed and throughput are critical, such as DeFi, NFTs and gaming. Its capacity for handling large volumes of transactions makes it well suited for markets requiring high-speed trading.

6. **Growing ecosystem:** The Solana ecosystem includes a growing number of projects across different sectors, including DeFi protocols, NFT marketplaces and decentralised exchanges (DEXs). This diverse range of applications contributes to its robustness and appeal as a platform for blockchain development.

Solana's architecture and performance characteristics make it a prominent choice for developers and organisations aiming to leverage blockchain technology for applications requiring high speed and scalability. Now let's take a look at Bitcoin.

BITCOIN

Bitcoin is the first and most widely recognised cryptocurrency, founded in 2009 by an individual or group using the pseudonym Satoshi Nakamoto. It is known for being the pioneer of blockchain technology, offering a decentralised solution to digital currency. Here are some key aspects of Bitcoin:

1. **Decentralisation**: Bitcoin operates on a decentralised network of computers (nodes) that validate and record

all transactions on the blockchain. This decentralisation ensures that no single entity has control over the entire Bitcoin network.

2. **Limited supply:** Bitcoin has a capped supply of 21 million coins, which helps to prevent inflation and contributes to its perception as digital gold. This scarcity is an essential aspect of its value proposition.

3. **Mining and security:** Bitcoin employs a consensus mechanism known as Proof of Work (PoW), where complex mathematical problems are solved by miners to authenticate transactions and secure the network. As a reward, miners receive newly minted bitcoins and transaction fees.

4. **Store of value and investment**: Often referred to as 'digital gold', Bitcoin is widely regarded as a store of value and a hedge against inflation, much like precious metals. Its independence from traditional financial systems makes it attractive to investors looking for an alternative asset class.

5. **Widespread adoption:** Bitcoin is the most recognised and extensively used cryptocurrency globally. It is accepted by numerous businesses for transactions and has spurred a vast ecosystem of other cryptocurrencies and blockchain projects.

6. **Volatility**: Despite its benefits, Bitcoin is known for its price volatility, which can cause significant fluctuations over short periods. This is ultimately influenced by a number of factors, including market sentiment, the global economic environment and regulatory news. Bitcoin continues to be a cornerstone of the cryptocurrency world, influencing numerous innovations in the digital and financial sectors. The introduction of ETFs for both Bitcoin and Ethereum has exponentially increased the monetary volumes flowing into the cryptocurrencies.

It also increases the level of safety and trust in investing in an ETF, which means it is managed for you while still benefiting in its upside potential. Its development over the years has been closely tied to the broader discussion about the idea that digital currencies are becoming closer to being a reality.

AVALANCHE

Avalanche is another leading blockchain platform, recognised for its revolutionary consensus mechanism known for its remarkable speed and scalability, making it a strong contender in the decentralised technology landscape. It supports diverse applications, including DeFi and digital collectibles as well as being positioned as a leader within blockchain gaming. Here are some key aspects of Avalanche:

1. **High throughput**: Avalanche can process thousands of transactions per second, positioning it as one of the fastest blockchains available. This capability is particularly advantageous for applications requiring quick transaction finality.

2. **Scalability**: The platform employs a unique consensus protocol known as the Avalanche consensus, which allows for rapid processing while maintaining strong security and decentralisation. This scalability makes it suitable for large-scale enterprise applications.

3. **Interoperability and flexibility:** Avalanche supports the creation of custom subnets, which are essentially private or public blockchains that can operate under their own rules within the Avalanche ecosystem. This feature enables high customisation and interoperability among different blockchain projects.

4. **Developer-friendly:** Avalanche is compatible with the Ethereum Virtual Machine (EVM), which allows developers to easily port existing Ethereum dApps onto the Avalanche network with minimal changes. This compatibility reduces the barrier to entry for developers familiar with Ethereum's development environment.

5. **Use cases:** The platform is widely used for DeFi applications, asset issuance and trading. Its capabilities also extend to other areas such as NFTs and gaming, where its high throughput and quick finality are critical.

6. **Growing ecosystem:** The Avalanche ecosystem includes a wide range of applications and services, from automated market makers (AMMs) and lending platforms to innovative financial products, contributing to its robust and rapidly growing community.

POLYGON

Polygon (formerly known as Matic Network) is a well-regarded blockchain platform that serves as a scaling solution for Ethereum. It is designed to address some of the main limitations of traditional blockchain networks, including poor user experience (high fees, slow transactions) and lack of community governance. Here are five of its key features and uses:

1. **Scalability**: Polygon provides multiple tools to enhance scalability using an adapted version of the Plasma framework. This framework provides a solution for faster and extremely low-cost transactions with finality on the main chain. It is built on proof-of-stake checkpoints that run through the Ethereum main chain.

2. **Ethereum compatibility**: Being a sidechain to Ethereum, Polygon is fully compatible with Ethereum's existing tools like MetaMask and supports all the existing Ethereum dApps. Developers can deploy Ethereum-compatible smart contracts on Polygon's PoS-secured side chain without any code changes.

3. **Infrastructure and dApp development:** Polygon not only offers scalability solutions but also supports infrastructure development, such as APIs and SDKs for developers, making it easier to build and connect dApps that can communicate both with Ethereum and other blockchain networks.

4. **Security**: The network leverages the security of Ethereum through a novel architecture involving validators and a system of checkpoints to ensure asset security even as transactions are processed quickly on side chains.

5. **Use cases**: Polygon is used for a variety of applications, primarily those that require faster transaction times and lower costs, such as gaming, DeFi and NFTs. It is particularly popular among developers looking to build scalable dApps that can operate efficiently at a fraction of the cost required on the Ethereum mainnet.

Polygon has been crucial in providing a more accessible and efficient environment for building and operating dApps, significantly contributing to the broader Ethereum ecosystem.

In summary, the blockchain landscape has significantly changed and seen extensive development progress since the heady heights of the bull run in 2021, when ETH was really the major player in town when it came to NFTs and had little competition. Now, liquidity (funds), eyeballs, attention and sentiment are being spread across many more destinations including Bitcoin, Solana, Avalanche, Polygon and even new entrants that have recently emerged, such as Base from Coinbase.

10　Future outlook

It is prescient to offer a perspective on the future outlook by rooting it in the following quote from November 2023, in NFT Now by Wylie Aronow, aka Gordon Goner, Co-founder of Yuga Labs, who became one of the key success drivers and figureheads of the space.

> NFTs became a household name when they were meant to be a pretty culturally niche thing. For example, there are parallels between the punk rock movement and NFTs. The Sex Pistols never dreamed of being a household name, and yet that's what happened. From the Pistols, we got the Clash and the Ramones (my all-time favourite band), and the music industry promoted and capitalised everything into the ground. So then the punk scene kind of collapsed under the weight of too much attention – what I mean is it was no longer cool. The original ethos was lost, and it became more about fashion. The scene didn't really revive itself on a mainstream level until pop punk bands like Green Day came along, and by then, it wasn't so much about a rejection of societal norms, but a feeling of irreverence for them. I guess my point is that, like everything, attention comes in cycles. Someone takes an unpopular thing and does something interesting and cool with it, and it gets adopted in the mainstream, and it becomes uncool again. Rinse and repeat forever. I think NFTs are here to stay.[48]

---

48 LorePunk (2023) *Exclusive: Inside BAYC co-founder Gordon Goner's …*, *NFTNow*. Available at: https://nftnow.com/features/exclusive-inside-bayc-co-founder-gordon-goners-nft-shopping-spree.

Attention comes in cycles, and NFTs have been at the forefront of this new attention cycle in the past few years. I believe that NFTs are and will continue to be attention, momentum and cultural tokens. As with any brand building, the hardest part is consistency, purpose for its existence, utility and value that keeps people coming back.

But critically, for brands to succeed, they must not just focus on NFTs within the web3 ecosystem. In order to fully utilise the medium, data and insights, tokenisation, gaming, community-led immersive commerce and in-person events, real-world activations, not to forget AI and generative AI should all be harnessed, combined and act as multipliers together.

Out of all this, if we end up with the belief that NFTs are ultimately attention tokens and culture has the ability to be tokenised forever, you then have to wonder what legacy these projects leave. Which ones will continue to survive, thrive and flourish and which will never be seen again?

At the time of writing, in Q2 2024, CryptoPunks remains the gold standard project, currently standing at a 36 ETH floor price (but even it suffered an initial sentiment wobble after introducing the 'Super Punk World' derivative with Nina Chanel in May 2024). Beeple has cemented its place in history for kicking off a lot of the hype and excitement around the space with its $69 million sale by Christie's in March 2021. Pudgy Penguins has sold over 1 million plushies in Walmart stores in the USA. Autoglyphs by Larva Labs will always remain the first on-chain generative art project on the Ethereum blockchain and like Beeple, will cement its place in history as a result. Squiggles are unashamedly culture and an in-the-know (ITK) nod to generative art (see cultural capital in Chapter 6).

Fidenza by Tyler Hobbs (42 ETH), Ringers by Dmitri Cherniak (20 ETH), Gazers by Matt Kane (8 ETH), Meridian by Matt DesLauriers (4 ETH) and Winds of Yawanawa by Refik Anadol (4 ETH) from the generative art world will all be remembered, loved and sought after for years to come, for being part of a key snapshot in time where artistic craft, technical wizardry and algorithmic genius prevailed over short-termism.

Doodles is to release a short film, *Dullsville and the Doodleverse*, in September 2024 with an immersive experience launch at the Toronto International Film Festival, followed by a global release. Azuki is creating a world experience around the $ANIME token and CryptoPunks is releasing a book with PHAIDON 'Free To Claim' with versions for holders and fans, chronicling its story and history.

Yuga Labs will release its Fortnite/Roblox-esque online gaming world, called Otherside, where you will be able to be part of the gaming world as one of the IPs of the Yuga Labs universe, for example, Bored Apes, Mutants, Meebits, Moonbirds and more. In February 2024, Meebits released its own world inside Otherside, called Meetropolis, inviting its most ardent supporters to a private viewing and playtest weekend in Berlin, Germany, where each attendee, some of whom had travelled from across the globe, had their Meebit fully rigged as a playable 3D model within the game world and were able to play as their own Meebit character within the game.

RTFKT will release its physical sneakers to the world in the summer of 2024. I'm sure many surprise technical innovations that have not yet been announced will be integrated into the shoes.

What are we going to see more of across Q4 2024, 2025 and beyond? I hope to see a greater acceptance and appreciation of NFTs and further linkage with web3 and smart contracts combined with AI. This is going to be the ultimate defence mechanism against deep fakes, fake news and lies within the media. As well as defamatory content that is purported to have been created by a brand, and particularly given the political landscape in the USA, UK and beyond in 2024, being able to trust what we see, hear and read is going to be increasingly difficult without proper authentication at source. If we were to imagine what the Nielsen for digital media would look like, trust in content will go up, our belief system will shift from what is currently untrusting, wary, unsure and perhaps even a little on the pessimistic side, with a positive effect for humanity.

What does the future hold for NFTs specifically? I think we will see a small percentage of the cream rising to the top and having staying power, with a large consolidation of projects over the next year, meaning that some will cease to exist. There were many opportunist people, influencers, projects and brands who made some short-term money and quickly exited. Coupled with the overarching volatility of crypto and the increasing fervour around AI, it requires a long-term, pragmatic approach with a purpose rather than just seeking to make a quick buck. That era is hopefully behind us after the shiny newness fades. Now, I expect to see less volume, less activity than the bull run times but more longer-termism, more commitment to programmes over launches and a greater sense of depth.

What does Julian Holguin from Doodles think is the future of brands and content in an increasingly tokenised world?

> *Producing great content, incentivizing co-creation and tokenizing attention/fandom = the future of media development. A future where value accrual shifts from the publisher & distributor to the creator and their community. Consumer crypto will have a profound impact on media.*[49]

Meanwhile, as Wylie Aronow said, 'I think NFTs are here to stay.'[50] I agree that the underpinning tech will stay and thrive but how we interface with it, engage with the front end and transact is all still open to change. Ledger Stax is going to change how we interface with a security device. I think the same is going to need to happen with the NFT industry. The ease of onboarding, the user experience, the ability to seamlessly use offline payment methods such as credit cards coupled with crypto will all get better, easier, cheaper, faster and less complex in the coming years. Maybe NFTs themselves

---

49 *X.com* (2024a) *X (formerly Twitter)*. Available at: https://x.com/jholguin/status/1794536481756995900?s=46.

50 LorePunk (2023) *Exclusive: Inside BAYC co-founder Gordon Goner's ...*, *NFTNow*. Available at: https://nftnow.com/features/exclusive-inside-bayc-co-founder-gordon-goners-nft-shopping-spree.

will even get a rebrand. Digital collectibles, for example, seem much more easily understandable to me.

Thinking through an art lens, as Damien Hirst put it during the height of his 'Currency' NFT project fame, 'Art is about making art for people who haven't been born yet'.[51] Perhaps the same will remain true for NFTs and there will continue to be many new chapters for NFTs in 2025 and beyond.

And finally, an apt way to finish: 'I love the idea of community but I also love the idea of survival and when you're surviving that's the most exciting thing for me', says Damien Hirst in *NFT: WTF?* for Netflix, 2024.[52]

NFTs arrived, thrived and so far have survived, but what may be in store for us and their next chapter of reinvention? That chapter remains unwritten. Tweet me and let me know what you think @mlitman!

51 *Watch NFT: WTF?* (2024) *Netflix.* Available at: www.netflix.com/gb/title/81734936.

52 Ibid.

Abbreviations

AI	artificial intelligence
AMM	automated market makers
BIMA	British Interactive Media Association
DAO	decentralised autonomous organisation
dApp	decentralised application
DEX	decentralised exchange
ETF	exchange-traded fund
EVM	Ethereum Virtual Machine
ITK	in the know
KPMG	Klynveld Peat Marwick Goerdeler
NFC	near-field communication
NFT	non-fungible token
NYU	New York University
PFP	profile picture project
POAP	proof of attendance protocol
PoH	proof of history
PoS	proof of stake
QR code	quick response code
RFID	radio frequency identification
TLA	Tech London Advocates
TPS	transaction per second

Glossary

Airdrop: A distribution of cryptocurrency tokens or NFTs to users, typically for free, as a way to promote a new project or reward loyal community members.

Bitcoin: A decentralised digital currency that operates without a central bank, using blockchain technology to enable peer-to-peer transactions.

Blockchain: A distributed ledger technology that records transactions across a network of computers in a secure and transparent manner, forming a chain of blocks.

Bridging: The process of transferring assets or data from one blockchain to another, typically using a cross-chain bridge to facilitate interoperability between different blockchain networks.

Burning (burn/burned): The process of permanently removing tokens from circulation by sending them to an address from which they cannot be retrieved, often used to reduce the supply of a token or NFT.

Cold wallet: A cryptocurrency wallet that is kept offline to provide a higher level of security, used primarily for long-term storage of assets.

Collectible: An item that is valued and collected for its rarity, uniqueness or cultural significance, often with potential for appreciation in value.

Cross-chain: Refers to the ability of different blockchain networks to interact with each other, allowing assets and data to be transferred across chains.

Crypto wallet: A digital wallet used to store, send and receive cryptocurrencies, often secured with private keys.

Cryptocurrency: A digital or virtual currency that uses cryptography for security and operates on decentralised networks, typically using blockchain technology.

Cultural capital: The non-financial social assets that promote social mobility, such as education, intellect, style of speech, dress or physical appearance.

Custodial wallet: A type of cryptocurrency wallet where a third party holds and manages the user's private keys, similar to how a bank holds and manages money for a user.

DAO (Decentralised Autonomous Organisation): An organisation represented by rules encoded as a computer program that is transparent, controlled by members of the organisation, and not influenced by a central government.

DAPP: An application that runs on a decentralised network, typically using blockchain technology, without a centralised authority.

DeFi (Decentralised Finance): A financial ecosystem that operates on blockchain technology, removing intermediaries like banks and brokers to create a more open, accessible financial system.

DEX (Decentralised Exchange): A peer-to-peer marketplace where transactions occur directly between crypto traders without needing a central authority or intermediary.

Doxxing: The act of publicly revealing personal information about an individual without their consent, often with malicious intent.

Dusting attack: A type of cyberattack where small amounts of cryptocurrency are sent to wallets in an attempt to trace and de-anonymize the wallet owners.

Ecosystem: A complex network or interconnected system, in this context often referring to the environment surrounding cryptocurrencies or blockchain technology, including users, developers, and institutions.

ENS (Ethereum Name Service): A decentralised naming service that maps human-readable names like yourname.eth to machine-readable identifiers, such as Ethereum addresses.

ERC-721: A standard for representing ownership of non-fungible tokens (NFTs) on the Ethereum blockchain. Each token is unique and not interchangeable.

ERC-1155: A multi-token standard that allows for the creation of both fungible and non-fungible tokens within the same smart contract. It is more efficient than ERC-721, especially for gaming applications.

ETF (Exchange-Traded Fund): A type of security that involves a collection of securities—such as stocks—that often tracks an underlying index, though they can invest in any number of industry sectors or use various strategies.

Ethereum: A decentralised platform that enables smart contracts and decentralised applications (dApps) to be built and run without any downtime, fraud or control by a third party, using its own cryptocurrency called Ether (ETH).

EVM (Ethereum Virtual Machine): The runtime environment for smart contracts in Ethereum. It is responsible for executing the bytecode of Ethereum's smart contracts.

Floor price: The lowest price at which an NFT from a particular collection is currently listed for sale on a marketplace.

FOMO (Fear of Missing Out): A psychological phenomenon in the crypto and NFT space where investors feel pressure to buy into a project or asset due to its rising popularity or value, fearing they might miss out on potential profits.

Fractionalisation: The process of dividing an asset into smaller, fractional shares, allowing multiple people to own a portion of the asset, often used in the context of NFTs or real estate.

Gas fee: A fee required to conduct a transaction or execute a contract most famously on the Ethereum blockchain. This fee compensates miners for the computational power needed to process and validate transactions.

Gas wars: A situation where transaction fees on a blockchain increase dramatically due to high demand, often occurring during popular NFT drops or other high-traffic events on networks like Ethereum.

Generative art: Art that is created using algorithms or autonomous systems, often involving randomness or computer code, resulting in unique and often digital works.

Governance token: A type of cryptocurrency that gives holders the right to participate in the decision-making process of a blockchain protocol, usually through voting on proposals.

Hot wallet: A cryptocurrency wallet that is connected to the internet, making it more convenient for frequent transactions but also more vulnerable to hacks.

Interoperability: The ability of different systems, platforms, or applications to work together seamlessly, often referring to the ability of blockchain networks or software to interact and share information.

Layer 1: Refers to the base layer of a blockchain, such as Bitcoin or Ethereum, that operates independently and is responsible for processing and validating transactions.

Layer 2: Solutions or protocols built on top of a blockchain (like Ethereum) to improve scalability and reduce transaction costs by handling transactions off the main blockchain before settling them back onto the main chain.

Liquidity pool: A collection of funds locked in a smart contract, used to facilitate trading by providing liquidity in decentralised exchanges (DEXs) and other DeFi platforms.

Marketplace: A platform where goods, services, or digital assets like NFTs are bought and sold, often decentralised and using blockchain technology in the context of cryptocurrency.

Metamask: A popular browser extension and mobile app that functions as a cryptocurrency wallet, allowing users to interact with decentralised applications (dApps) across blockchains.

Metaverse: A collective virtual shared space, created by the convergence of virtually enhanced physical reality and persistent virtual reality, often involving augmented reality, virtual reality, and blockchain technologies.

MEV (Miner Extractable Value): The maximum value that miners or validators can extract from block production beyond standard block rewards and gas fees, often by reordering, including, or excluding transactions.

Minting: The process of creating a new NFT and recording it on the blockchain. This process often involves paying a gas fee and results in the generation of a unique digital asset.

Multisignature wallet (Multisig): A type of digital wallet that requires multiple private keys to authorise a transaction, adding an extra layer of security by distributing control among multiple parties.

NFC (Near-Field Communication): A set of communication protocols that enable two electronic devices to establish communication by bringing them within a few centimetres of each other.

Node: A computer that participates in a blockchain network by validating and relaying transactions. Nodes maintain the network's ledger and contribute to its decentralisation and security.

Non-custodial wallet: A wallet where the user has full control over their private keys, meaning they have full control over their cryptocurrency and are responsible for its security.

Non-fungible token: A unique digital asset that represents ownership or proof of authenticity of a specific item, often used for digital art, collectibles, and other media, and is not interchangeable like cryptocurrencies.

Oracle: A service that provides external data to smart contracts, enabling them to interact with real-world events or information outside of the blockchain.

Paper hands: A slang term for an investor who sells their assets at the first sign of trouble, typically used to contrast with 'diamond hands', who hold onto their investments despite volatility.

Peer-to-peer: A decentralised network where two or more computers or devices interact directly with each other without the need for a central server or intermediary.

PFP NFT (Profile Picture Projects): A type of NFT that is primarily used as a profile picture on social media platforms, often representing membership and tribalism in a digital community or having collectible value.

Phygital: A blend of physical and digital experiences, where physical objects or events are enhanced with digital elements, often involving interactive technology or blockchain.

POAP (Proof of Attendance Protocol): A protocol that allows users to collect badges or tokens that serve as proof of their attendance at an event, often associated with physical or virtual events.

PoH (Proof of History): A cryptographic technique that enables the verification of the passage of time between events, commonly used in blockchain systems.

PoS (Proof of Stake): A consensus mechanism for blockchains that selects validators in proportion to their quantity of holdings in the associated cryptocurrency.

PoW (Proof of Work): A consensus mechanism used in blockchain networks like Bitcoin, where complex mathematical problems are solved by miners to authenticate transactions and secure the network

Programmability: The ability to create and execute automated and customisable processes or logic, often referring to smart contracts in blockchain technology that self-execute when conditions are met.

Provenance: The documented history of an asset's ownership, origin, and authenticity, often tracked using blockchain technology for transparency and verification, especially for art and collectibles.

RFID (Radio-Frequency Identification): A technology that uses electromagnetic fields to automatically identify and track tags attached to objects.

Rug pull: A type of scam in the cryptocurrency and NFT space where developers of a project abruptly withdraw funds, abandoning the project and leaving investors with worthless assets.

Seed phrase: A series of words generated when a wallet is created, used to recover the private key and access the cryptocurrency stored in the wallet.

Self-custody: The practice of managing and controlling your own cryptocurrency or NFTs without relying on third-party services, typically done using a non-custodial wallet.

Sharding: A method of splitting a blockchain into smaller, more manageable pieces (shards) to improve scalability and efficiency by processing transactions in parallel across multiple shards.

Smart contracts: Self-executing contracts with the terms directly written into code, running on blockchain networks, automatically enforcing and executing agreements when predefined conditions are met.

Snapshot: A record of the state of a blockchain at a specific point in time, often used in governance voting or to determine eligibility for airdrops.

Sniping: The practice of quickly buying an underpriced NFT or token from a marketplace, often using automated tools or bots to gain an advantage.

Soulbound tokens (SBTs): A type of NFT that is non-transferable and permanently bound to a wallet, often used to represent personal achievements, credentials or identity.

Staking: The process of participating in a proof-of-stake (PoS) blockchain by locking up cryptocurrency in a wallet to support network operations like validating transactions, often earning rewards in return.

Tokenisation: The process of converting rights or ownership of a physical or digital asset into a digital token that can be bought, sold, or traded on a blockchain.

Tokenomics: The economic structure of a cryptocurrency or token, including aspects like its distribution, supply, demand and use cases within its ecosystem.

Transaction per second (TPS): A metric used to measure the speed of a blockchain network, representing the number of transactions that can be processed per second

Wash trading: An illegal practice where a trader buys and sells the same asset to create misleading activity in the market, artificially inflating its price or volume.

Whale: A term used to describe an individual or entity that holds a large amount of cryptocurrency or NFTs, capable of influencing market prices due to their significant holdings.

Whitelisting: The process of giving pre-approved users access to a particular event or sale, commonly used in NFT drops to allow certain users to buy tokens before the general public.

Wrapped token: A token that represents another cryptocurrency or asset on a different blockchain, allowing it to be used on that blockchain while maintaining the value of the original asset.

Yield farming: The practice of earning interest or additional tokens by lending or staking cryptocurrency in decentralised finance (DeFi) protocols.

Zero-Knowledge Proof (ZKP): A cryptographic method by which one party can prove to another that a statement is true without revealing any specific information about the statement itself, often used to enhance privacy in blockchain transactions.

Published by BCS Learning & Development Ltd, a wholly owned subsidiary of BCS, The Chartered Institute for IT, 3 Newbridge Square, Swindon, SN1 1BY, UK.
www.bcs.org

Paperback ISBN: 978-1-78017-6499
PDF ISBN: 978-1-78017-6505
ePUB ISBN: 978-1-78017-6512

Ebook
available

British Cataloguing in Publication Data.
A CIP catalogue record for this book is available at the British Library.

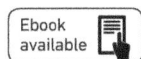

Disclaimer:

Publisher's acknowledgements
Reviewers: Rhian Lewis and Adel ElMessiry
Publisher: Ian Borthwick
Commissioning editor: Heather Wood
Production manager: Florence Leroy
Project manager: Just Content Ltd
Copy-editor: Just Content Ltd
Proofreader: Just Content Ltd
Cover design: Alex Wright
Cover image: iStock - StationaryTraveller
Sales director: Charles Rumball
Typeset by Lapiz Digital Services, Chennai, India

BCS, THE CHARTERED INSTITUTE FOR IT

BCS, The Chartered Institute for IT, is committed to making IT good for society. We use the power of our network to bring about positive, tangible change. We champion the global IT profession and the interests of individuals, engaged in that profession, for the benefit of all.

Exchanging IT expertise and knowledge
The Institute fosters links between experts from industry, academia and business to promote new thinking, education and knowledge sharing.

Supporting practitioners
Through continuing professional development and a series of respected IT qualifications, the Institute seeks to promote professional practice tuned to the demands of business. It provides practical support and information services to its members and volunteer communities around the world.

Setting standards and frameworks
The Institute collaborates with government, industry and relevant bodies to establish good working practices, codes of conduct, skills frameworks and common standards. It also offers a range of consultancy services to employers to help them adopt best practice.

Become a member
Over 70,000 people including students, teachers, professionals and practitioners enjoy the benefits of BCS membership. These include access to an international community, invitations to a roster of local and national events, career development tools and a quarterly thought-leadership magazine. Visit https://www.bcs.org to find out more.

Learn more about BCS qualifications and certifications at https://certifications.bcs.org/

Further information
BCS, The Chartered Institute for IT,
3 Newbridge Square, Swindon, SN1 1BY, UK.
T +44 (0) 1793 417 417
(Monday to Friday, 09:00 to 17:00 UK time)
www.bcs.org/contact
http://shop.bcs.org/
publishing@bcs.uk

www.ingramcontent.com/pod-product-compliance
Lightning Source LLC
Chambersburg PA
CBHW042118190326
41519CB00030B/7540